LIFE'S LIKE THAT
Meeting God in the everyday

JEANETTE HENDERSON

To Nicola, Lynsey, Amy,
Sean and Alexander
With love

Scripture Union, 207–209 Queensway, Bletchley, MK2 2EB, England.

© Jeanette Henderson 1999

First published 1999

ISBN 1 85999 311 7

British Library Cataloguing-in-Publication Data
A catalogue record for this book is available from the British Library.

Cover design by The Big Picture.
Printed and bound in Great Britain by Creative Print and Design, (Wales) Ebbw Vale.

CONTENTS

INTRODUCTION

I was accompanying my sister and her family on their weekly visit to the local supermarket. As she and my nephew, Sean, dashed about filling their trolley with food, her husband kept fourteen-month-old Amy entertained. I watched as father and daughter sauntered at snail's pace around the store, my brother-in-law bent almost double, one finger held tightly by a chubby little hand, while Amy tottered along quite cheerfully at his side. As they went, Daddy chatted to her, happily pointing things out along the way, patiently explaining – in 'toddler talk', of course! – all that was going on around them, turning an ordinary, mundane chore, believe it or not, into a valuable learning experience.

I hadn't been a child of God for long when I realised that this is how it can be in our relationship with the Lord. He is the God who leans down to meet us where we are. We don't have to stand on spiritual 'tiptoe' to reach him. He is with us wherever we are, whatever we're doing, even in the least exciting experiences of life. He is there when we drag ourselves out of bed in the morning, when we're up to the eyes in ironing or struggling to clean that nasty ring mark from around the bath. He is interested in every part of our lives and wants to be involved at every level. Nothing is insignificant – and neither are we!

In this book I share with you some of my own real-life experiences, showing how God can teach us in and through normal, everyday living as well as through his written word. He rarely separates scripture from ordinary life. In his parables, Jesus used as examples familiar sights and events to help his listeners understand and remember the biblical concepts he was teaching them. And it can be the same for us today.

Often, if I don't understand something written in his word, I tell the

Lord and ask him to show me more simply, practical examples from my normal environment. And that's exactly what he does.

The readings and reflections in this book are meant to be used in addition to your usual daily devotions, whenever you find you have a bit of time to spare. There is no strict time or pattern for reading: you can take each chapter individually, working through the 'Focus' and 'Feed' sections as you go; or you can have a bit of a binge by cramming the book as a whole and then going back to work through each chapter more slowly. Before you begin each time, prayerfully commit it to the Lord. It is a good idea to keep a pen and notebook handy beside your Bible, to note everything the Holy Spirit brings to mind. That's how this book came into being!

God the Father is already reaching down to meet you where you are, ready and very willing to take you by the hand and turn even the most mundane activities of life into experiences of learning about him. Why not accept his proffered hand now? Invite him to make you much more aware of what he wants to teach you through the everyday things around you. Expressing your eagerness to learn in this way is the first step: the next is giving the Lord daily permission to make your willingness a reality. Go on, give it a try. It's exciting. Honestly!

1

'WILL YOU JOIN ME?'

One of the busiest days of my life so far has to be the day when my youngest sister, Gillian, was married. I was chief bridesmaid. Well, that's what I started out as. In the hours before the actual ceremony, however, I ended up with a few other jobs to do as well.

Almost immediately, I became chief cook and bottle washer, maker of numerous drinks for the many visitors who popped in to say hello. As the bride's personal secretary, I noted the dozens of phone messages from well-wishers. I was elected personal chauffeur to the bride's (and my) mother when she decided she just had to do some last-minute shopping. As the all-important child-minder, I made sure that the page boy and flower girl stopped squabbling and behaved themselves for a few hours at least! I was the messenger who chased up a late delivery of flowers. And, last but not least, as the bride's very own confidante, I had to calm and counsel her when last-minute nerves almost caused her to cancel everything. (I think I actually told her that she was going to be married that day even if I had to carry her screaming up the aisle!)

I was extremely busy and bowed down with responsibility. I had no time to spare the entire morning, with the result that when the limousine came to escort my mother, the other bridesmaids and myself to church, I was still dressed in jeans and an old jumper, having helped everyone else to get ready.

Now let me tell you about my dad that day. He had already seen two of his other daughters married not so many months before. So, as 'father of the bride' once again, he knew already exactly what was expected of him and exactly when it was required. In the middle of all the hustle and bustle – as the bride and bridesmaids (and my mother.) had their hair done, faces made up, posh dresses put on, and so on –

my father sneaked out of the sitting room, found the most comfortable armchair and ensconced himself on it in a quiet corner of the kitchen, well out of everyone's way. On one side he lined up his favourite pipes, and on the other he set out everything required for drinks and snacks. In front of him, he laid his newspaper, crossword puzzle book, current paperback and radio.

I remember that at one stage during the course of my many duties, when I had rushed past him for the hundredth time, he looked up from his newspaper, grinned at me and said, 'I've just made a pot of tea and some buttered toast, Jeanette. Will you join me?'

'Join you! Join you!' I replied, frustration absolutely oozing from my ears. 'Have you seen all that I still have to do before we even get to the church? I'm sorry, Dad, but I really don't have time to join you!'

'Fair enough!' he said, shrugging his shoulders and returning to his newspaper.

Do you know that, twelve years later, I regret not accepting my father's invitation? On many occasions since then, I have wished that I had made time to sit and sup tea with him, even if for only a few minutes – it would have made such a tremendous difference to the rest of my day. You see, as he escorted my sister up the aisle, my father looked relaxed, happy and very distinguished. While I resembled someone who had just run the London marathon! I have to confess that the rest of the day was a struggle to enjoy, even though we Scots know how to celebrate.

> Jesus said, 'Here I am! I stand at the door and knock. If anyone hears my voice and opens the door, I will come in and eat with him, and he with me.'
>
> *(Revelation 3:20)*

We often quote this verse to people who aren't Christians, when we are talking with them about salvation. However, it was actually directed at Christians in the church of Laodicea, a church whose faith and zeal had become lukewarm.

Be honest now! How many times do we hear the Lord Jesus knock and say, 'Will you join me?' and we find ourselves replying, 'Join you, Lord? Have you seen all that's still to be done? Sorry, but I just don't have time to join you!' On our busiest days, if we talked to our husband or best friend as little as we talk to the Lord, then many of us would be struggling to enjoy a successful marriage or friendship. And yet, seeing how easily we neglect to spend time regularly with Jesus, how can we honestly expect our relationship with him to succeed?

As a Bible college student I learned some very long words which I could barely say, never mind understand: words like 'post-exilic', 'ante-millennial' and – wait for it – 'eschatological'! Using them made me sound impressive – especially when invited to tea with the minister – but, honestly speaking, they meant very little to me because they touched my head and not my heart. One biblical word, however, which has become very precious to me over the years is, simply, the word '*come*'. When I consider the awesome character of the one who says it, compared to the awfulness of the one to whom it is said (namely, a sinner like myself), my heart just wants to sing over and over again, 'Thank you, Lord! Thank you!'

> 'Come now, let us reason together,'
>   says the Lord.
> 'Though your sins are like scarlet,
>   they shall be as white as snow;
> though they are red as crimson,
>   they shall be like wool.'
>
> *(Isaiah 1:18)*

> 'Come to me, all you who are weary and burdened, and I
> will give you rest. Take my yoke upon you and learn from
> me, for I am gentle and humble in heart, and you will
> find rest for your souls. For my yoke is easy and my
> burden is light.'
>
> *(Matthew 11:28–30)*

Several times in the course of an ordinary day, our extraordinary Lord will invite us to leave the hustle and bustle of our busyness to spend a few moments alone with him. Settle it now in your heart and mind that you will hear and heed his call. It will make such a tremendous difference to the rest of your day.

Focus

Ask the Holy Spirit to help you discover how you might rearrange your day in a practical way so that you can more readily accept the Lord's invitation to join him.

Then, at various times of the day, for example as you sit down with your mid-morning cup of coffee or drive home from work or to the supermarket, imagine Jesus there with you. Chat with him as you would a friend. Enjoy being with him, spending time in his company. Bring no 'prayer lists' or 'hidden agendas'.

Feed

Read Luke 10:38–42.

Jesus is in Bethany, a guest in the home of Martha, Mary and Lazarus. The custom was for the women of the household to prepare and serve the meal while the men sat and entertained the guests. Mary, however, had other ideas!

- What is Martha's priority here? How does Mary's priority differ?
- From his reply in verses 41–42, which of the two does Jesus seem to regard as the more necessary priority?
- If Martha had adopted the same priority as Mary, and the meal had been late or less sumptuous, do you think Jesus would have minded?
- Which is your greater priority, 'being with' Jesus or 'doing for' him? How can you change things to correct the balance?

Read John 12:2–8.
- Could Mary's sensitivity at this time, so near to Jesus' death, have developed out of the 'quality time' she had spent with him on his visits to their home?
- In what ways does your 'quality time' with Jesus enhance your personal worship of him?

2

LIFE'S LITTLE IRONIES

Hands up those of you who have a memory like a sieve! Come on now, don't be shy!

You are not on your own. In fact, if you're like me, you'll have to admit that your memory is more like a giant's fishing net! You don't believe me? Then just quiz some of the children in the school where I work. They'll tell you. There I am, telling them off for something. I get half way (if I'm blessed!) through a meaningful monologue on the merits of good behaviour, only to find that (a) the end of the sentence suddenly deserts me, leaving me drowning in a sea of 'ums' and 'ers' (not cool as far as playground cred is concerned), or (b) I can't remember why I'm telling them off in the first place (even more uncool cred-wise). Still, the little darlings (bless 'em) have learned to smile and nod tolerantly, saying, 'Yes, miss! Sorry, miss!' to my face, while silently and sympathetically mouthing behind my back, 'It's her age, poor soul!'

In reality, and I am embarrassed to admit it, it has nothing to do with my age. I have always been like this. What's more, as well as sporting a pathetic memory, I have an even worse reputation for losing things. You're familiar with the drill, I'm sure. I lay something down safely somewhere and, within minutes, it has been whisked off by aliens – either that or I have forgotten where I've put it! Friends are forever teasing me. They have mischievously worked out that if they were to gather together under one roof all the things I have misplaced over the years, they would need a very large hall to put it all in – and they'd be right. You name it, I have probably lost it at some time or other. Included among the items I've mislaid would have to be my car: too many times in the past, I have forgotten where I've parked it!

Recently, I sat down and tried to recall the many other 'victims' of my appalling memory – the countless umbrellas, handbags, purses, jackets, books, pens, keys... I could go on for hours! They would certainly take up a great deal of room.

What about the 'lost' things which can't be gathered together? Things like the many competitions and games I have lost over the years (my eight-year-old niece, Lynsey, still trounces me at Snakes and Ladders!). How often in the past have I foolishly lost time? Or the times, during school exams, when I nervously lost facts. ('When was the Battle of Hastings?' 'How do you say "sausages" in French?' ... I knew it a minute ago.) And the times when I have 'lost my head' with sheer excitement (usually on the terraces at Murrayfield, watching Scotland win at rugby? OK, OK, so it doesn't happen often these days.). Then, at college, I lazily lost marks and, as a result, lost prizes and awards. Of course, I have also lost my temper and, along with it, fairweather friends and allies.

Coming right up to date, what about the many times I've lost my way and ended up heading in the wrong direction? A helpful little tip for you: any major European city in which my mate Jenny and I haven't been lost just isn't worth visiting! (Guess which one's the navigator?)

On second thoughts, if my friends did try to gather together all that I have lost over the years, they would probably need something the size of the Barbican to store it all in!

One of the little ironies of life, which I really must share with you, is that during my vacations from college I actually used to work in the Lost Property office of our local bus station. Honestly! And some of the items people would come looking for left me feeling like a complete novice. There were electric kettles, buckets of live maggots (I kid you not), lost cats, dogs, and a parrot called Percy who used to swear like a trooper in three different languages, ironing boards, bagpipes and, on one occasion, someone came to claim a box of kippers two whole days after he'd left it behind on a bus. Whew, were we glad to be rid of those!

Then one day an old lady called Madge came looking for her only set of 'fawsh teesh'. She had searched everywhere for them and was 'deshparately upshet' when we were unable to help her. I can still picture her look of 'dishappoint...' – sorry, disappointment – as she trundled off home. A week later, however, she returned sporting a beautiful, bright, tooth-filled smile. We listened with delight as she described how her granddaughter had found them in the sugar bowl! (Did I mention that Madge was a teensy bit short-sighted?)

Now, have you noticed yet that it isn't just life which is full of little ironies? Even the Bible has its fair share!

'For my thoughts are not your thoughts,
neither are your ways my ways,' declares the Lord.
'As the heavens are higher than the earth,
so are my ways higher than your ways
and my thoughts than your thoughts.'

(Isaiah 55:8–9)

I am glad, actually, that this point is made so clearly to us, because as I read God's word I see so often how he chooses, acts and makes decisions in ways that I certainly wouldn't, were I in his place. This is where the Bible's little ironies come to light.

For instance, if you were planning the birth of the next member of the family into which the future Saviour of the world would be born centuries later, would you choose as parents two senior citizens, one of whom is known to be barren and whose combined ages already totalled 190 years? Yet God chose Abraham and Sarah to bring Isaac into the world!

What about when choosing someone to confront the mighty Pharaoh of Egypt to demand the release of hundreds of thousands of Hebrew slaves, and then to lead these slaves bravely and wisely for forty years in the desert? Would Moses have been your ideal choice – a man who had grown up in luxury and comfort as an Egyptian prince, who then became a fugitive wanted for murder, who was painfully aware of his poor communication skills? However, Moses was God's choice!

Would you think of sending a young lad, armed only with a home-made catapult and five tiny pebbles, into mortal combat with a fully-armoured and fully-armed giant? But – yes, you've guessed it! – God chose young David to defeat Goliath!

Coming right into the New Testament, when assessing suitable candidates for the post of 'disciple', would you have picked any of the men Jesus chose? Had we been seeking to appoint potential companions and co-workers for the Son of God, we would have made straight for the local synagogues and interviewed their most learned, most religiously devoted students. From there, we would have gone to Jerusalem's finest royal courts to check out available millionaires and noblemen. But where did Jesus go? To the beaches, into the streets and marketplaces, among ordinary people of no social standing. His final choice consisted of the most unlikely characters – rough and

ready fishermen who were well-used to uttering curses and swear-
words, a highly unpopular customs-and-excise official in the employ of
the Romans and not above accepting a bribe or two to turn a blind eye
to smuggling, a couple of intensely-motivated members of an extremely militant political party, and so on. Yet these twelve men were willing to leave everything to follow Jesus and to listen to and absorb all
that he taught them. They watched as he healed the sick and disabled,
or freed people from evil spirits (see Luke 4:38–41). They witnessed the
mighty supernatural signs that he performed (see John 2:1–11;
6:1–24). And they watched these not from way up at the back of the
gallery but from right by Jesus' side. That close! And all the time they
spent in his company, they became more sensitive, more mature in
spirit, stronger in confidence, deeper in devotion, more ready to go out
on their own into the community to spread the good news of the
gospel:

> They [the disciples] went out and preached that people
> should repent. They drove out many demons and anoint-
> ed many sick people with oil and healed them.
>
> *(Mark 6:12–13)*

Jesus took a bunch of raw recruits, taught them, trained them and
patiently believed in them enough to see them moulded into the evan-
gelistic team which history records as having 'turned the known world
upside down'.

Are you feeling insignificant today? Totally inadequate for the task
you feel called to achieve for God? Then be encouraged by another little biblical irony which Paul reveals in one of his letters:

> To keep me from becoming conceited because of these
> surpassingly great revelations, there was given me a
> thorn in my flesh, a messenger of Satan, to torment me.
> Three times I pleaded with the Lord to take it away from
> me. But he said to me, 'My grace is sufficient for you, for
> my power is made perfect in weakness.' Therefore I will
> boast all the more gladly about my weaknesses, so that
> Christ's power may rest on me. That is why, for Christ's
> sake, I delight in weaknesses, in insults, in hardships, in
> persecutions, in difficulties. For when I am weak, then I
> am strong.
>
> *(2 Corinthians 12:7–10)*

When are we at our most powerful and fruitful in our Christian lives? Ironically, it is when we acknowledge and confess the very weaknesses we think make us inadequate; when we realise and admit the need for complete reliance on God, then humbly invite the Holy Spirit to work in us and through us according to his own all-powerful ability. So be encouraged! God hasn't finished with you yet, no matter how you may be feeling. He hasn't given up on me either, appalling memory and all! Praise his name!

Meanwhile, I'm struggling to solve the latest in life's little ironies. Bearing in mind my vast experience and expertise, why can't I lose the things that I really want to be rid of? Things like the huge 'crow's feet' lurking around my eyes; or the colourful boil which so thoughtfully appears on my chin the second I even look at a chocolate bar. And what about those awkward inches around my waist, which desperately must disappear if I am to look good in my new denims? Why, oh why, can't I lose any of these? Deep, burning issues, I know, which I will studiously ponder and inwardly digest until I finally unravel the answers. Meanwhile, what was the question again?

Focus

Invite the Holy Spirit to bring back to memory times in the past when you felt inadequate as a Christian but God still used you fruitfully to fulfil his plan and purposes. How did you feel in your success?

In response to his grace and faithfulness, offer your thanks and praise. Assure him of your willingness to be used again in the future.

Feed

Moses grew up as an Egyptian prince and fled to Midian after killing one of Pharaoh's soldiers. For the past forty years he has worked as a shepherd, looking after flocks owned by his father-in-law, Jethro. God, however, now has other plans for him.

Read Exodus 3:1 – 4:17.

Moses is not keen to do what God is asking of him. In reply, he offers five excuses (3:11,13; 4:1,10,13).

- Identify each excuse. How does God respond in each case? (3:12,14–15; 4:2–9,11–17)
- When you are not keen to do something the Lord asks of you, how creative can you become in the excuses you make? How does he usually respond to these?

3

OUR HANDS-ON GOD

What do woks, wedding rings, washing-up liquid and wallpaper all have in common – apart from the obvious? They all require the services of highly paid 'hand' models to advertise them. I should say extremely highly paid models, who can earn up to a thousand pounds a day just for allowing the cameras to photograph their perfectly formed hands. How many hours, I wonder, do they spend pampering and preening them? How many lorry loads of moisturising lotion and nail varnish does it take to keep them in tip-top condition? And how many thousands of pounds does it cost to insure them? Then, of course, there are many others who have remarkable hands – musicians, surgeons, artists, sportsmen and women. I wonder how much the tennis player Steffi Graf pays to insure her hands?

As a lay worker, I am often asked, 'What does Jesus look like? How tall is he? What colour are his hair and eyes?' To be honest, the Gospel accounts say little about his physical features, but all of them mention his hands.

Now that's unusual, because, naturally speaking, there was nothing out-of-the-ordinary about Jesus' hands. As a carpenter, they would have been calloused and rough, definitely not the type wanted for washing-up commercials! Supernaturally speaking, however, they were so remarkable that, had Jesus still been with us physically today, someone somewhere would have insured his hands for millions! Why? Because they changed so wonderfully the lives of everyone they touched.

First, Jesus used his hands to repair damaged bodies. There are many eye-witness accounts recorded for us, but let's focus for a moment on one Luke describes for us in his Gospel (13:10–17). Imagine that you have constant and excruciating pain because the tiny vertebrae of your spine are twisted and deformed. Imagine not being able to straighten up when you wanted to, not being able to lift your head to gaze at the stars, not even to look up into the eyes of those speaking to you. Luke, himself a doctor, describes a woman who had been disabled like this for eighteen long years. No one had been able to offer her a cure. Then, one day, she had a one-to-one with Jesus:

> When Jesus saw her, he called her forward and said to
> her, 'Woman, you are set free from your infirmity.' Then
> he put his hands on her, and immediately she straight-
> ened up and praised God.

> *(Luke 13:12)*

Over the years, since becoming a Christian, I have come to realise that it is not only damaged bones and bodies which Jesus can repair: he can also straighten out circumstances and schemes which have somehow become disjointed and confused. Certainly in my own life, his remarkable touch has unravelled many a tangled plan. And the result? Just like the woman in the story, I have much to thank God for!

Jesus used his hands to rescue those in trouble. In their eye-witness accounts, Matthew and John both tell of a particular night when they and the other disciples were sailing across a lake (Matthew 14:22–33); Luke 6:16–21). Four miles out from the shore, a fierce wind blew up and the waves began to toss them about. Terrified, they wished that Jesus was there to inspire courage in them, but he was still ashore and it was impossible to launch another boat in the storm. Yet Jesus had seen their struggle and was determined to reach them in their distress. It always amazes me how calmly the Gospel writers record how the disciples watched him coming towards them, walking on the lake's surface as though it were the most natural thing in the world! Stirred by this remarkable sight, impulsive Simon Peter climbed out of the boat to do the same. However, realising the strength of the wind against him, he became afraid and began to sink. 'Lord, save me!' he cried. Immediately, Jesus reached out his hand, caught hold of Peter and helped him back into the boat.

Jesus' hands were often busy performing amazing signs and wonders, for example when he took pity on a poor, grieving widow on the way to the funeral of her only son, and raised him back to life again (John 7:11–17). This and his many other miracles are all examples of 'high-powered' activities which either speeded up or suspended completely for a while the normal laws of nature as we know them. There is, however, an occasion recorded by John (13:1–17) where Jesus uses his hands to perform a more mundane task:

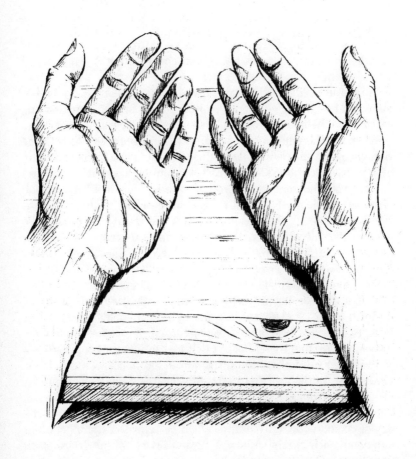

Having loved his own who were in the world, he now
showed them the full extent of his love ... he got up from
the meal, took off his outer clothing, and wrapped a towel
round his waist. After that, he poured water into a basin
and began to wash his disciples' feet, drying them with
the towel that was wrapped round him.

(John 13:1,4–5)

Here Jesus performed what would appear to be the least spectacular
act of his whole three year ministry on the earth, a task which should
have been performed by the lowest household servant. Yet it is in fact
one of the most powerfully significant.

And Jesus used his remarkable hands to reconcile broken relationships. To bridge the enormous gap caused by sin between God and
humankind, he allowed his hands, so often busy releasing health and
freedom into human lives, to be nailed to a rugged cross. As he hung
there in agony and near to death, the people standing by mocked him,
saying, 'He saved others but he can't save himself. If you really are who
you say you are, come down from that cross and we'll believe you!'
Here we see the most difficult thing Jesus ever had to do in his ministry, more difficult than healing the sick and raising the dead, more
difficult than defying gravity to walk on the surface of the sea. The
most difficult thing Jesus ever had to achieve, I believe, was *to make
himself stay on that cross*. He could have called legions of angels to
come and rescue him (Matthew 26:53), but he didn't. Instead, he made
himself stay there, facing insult, pain and finally death itself in order
to finish the work of reconciliation. It wasn't the nails that fastened
Jesus to the cross: it was his amazing, unselfish love for you and for
me which kept him there. Doesn't that make your heart rejoice?

Even after his death and resurrection, Jesus' hands were still busy.
The evening of the very first Easter Sunday, the disciples were hiding
in the upper room (John 20:19–29), when suddenly Jesus appeared.
Thomas, however, wasn't there (I suspect that keeping busy was his
way of coping with Jesus' death). When he returned, the others told
him about their special visitor. What was his response? 'Jesus? Back
from the dead? Standing in this very room, as if nothing's happened?
Give over! Unless I have tangible proof, I refuse to believe it.' Eight
days later, however, Jesus returned and gave Thomas exactly what he
asked for, offering his nail-pierced hands and saying, 'Thomas, stop
your doubting now and believe.' The response from Thomas is a
resounding declaration of faith – 'My Lord and my God!' – a declaration that would take him with the gospel message as far as India,

where he was finally martyred for the very faith he once thought had let him down.

I often find myself pondering why Jesus didn't use his hands that day to clip Thomas round the ears: 'Call yourself a disciple? I've seen more faith in a camel!' But he didn't. Gently and lovingly, he encouraged him back to faith.

Thus Jesus' hands were always busy ministering wholeness and freedom into the needy lives around him. His desire and expectation is that you and I will continue to do the same, in his precious name.

> 'I tell you the truth, anyone who has faith in me will do
> what I have been doing. He will do even greater things
> than these, because I am going to the Father.'
>
> *(John 14:12)*

Although Jesus is no longer physically here on the earth, those of us who commit ourselves to him in faith and trust are now his representatives. With the Holy Spirit's enabling, we are now his hands, feet, heart and smile in this needy world. Many have followed his example. Mother Theresa used her frail, old hands to tend the sores of dying beggars; there are others all over the world who have been moved to action by the love and compassion of our practical God.

Are your hands used to benefit and bless the lives of others? What you do doesn't always have to be a 'high-powered' miracle. Making a cup of tea for someone who is housebound, helping to share the burden of a neighbour's heavy shopping, offering a handshake of peace in a struggling relationship... No matter how unspectacular and mundane these may seem, when attempted in the name of Jesus and his great, unselfish love, they will count, practically and positively, for eternity. The Lord will make sure of that!

Focus
Have there been times in your own experience when others have blessed and encouraged you practically? Make a note of their names and brief details of what happened. In what ways did your life benefit by their kind actions?

Thank God for each name on your list and ask him to pour out his bountiful blessing on them today.

Feed
Read John 13:1–17.

Here we have an account of Jesus' last few hours with his disciples before his arrest and crucifixion. They are in the upper room, sharing a last meal together.

- What should always be the motivation for true servant-hood (v 1)?
- What other qualities make servanthood possible (v 3)?
- Are these qualities and motivation present in your own life as a Christian?

Read James 2:14–17.
- Ask the Holy Spirit to bring to mind those people around you who are in need. List their names and consider prayer-fully how you can help to meet these needs practically.
- Invite the Holy Spirit to give you opportunities to express your faith in positive action.

4

YEUCK!

Several years ago, my brother-in-law Brian was subjected to a horrific experience, the memory of which, he tells me, still makes him cringe to this day. Although he had anticipated and dreaded it for weeks beforehand, it actually happened a few days prior to his wedding. At the time he was a landscape gardener, working as part of a team which maintained the grounds of our local hospital. It has long been the custom in Scotland for a prank to be played by his workmates on a poor, innocent soul about to enter the blissful state of matrimony. In keeping with age-old tradition, Brian was grabbed by a half-dozen or so lads and duly stripped to his underwear. (I know that he was secretly relieved that he and Gillian had decided against a winter wedding. Not that it would have mattered if it had been winter – this same ritual would still have been carried out even in the middle of a snowstorm!)

He was then tied to a huge oak tree, where he had to stand helplessly while he was covered from head to foot by what can only be described as gooey gunge! All kinds of ingredients were thrown at him – raw eggs, rotten tomatoes, ketchup, salad cream, custard powder, sugar, coffee granules, various colours of powder paint, shoe polish, syrup, and so on. You name it, he was probably covered in it! He tells me that the worst thing he had to endure was having black treacle poured over his shoulder-length curly hair, on top of which was emptied a box of crushed cornflakes. (At the wedding reception, a score of showers later, Brian was still finding the odd crumb of cornflake!) You can imagine the mess he was in and how he felt as he was left there, tied to the tree for the rest of the day.

Months later, Brian admitted that this had been extremely unpleasant. However, what had been an even worse ordeal was the waiting, for days beforehand, wondering where, when and how it was going to happen. He had witnessed other workmates suffering in the same way just before they had married. In fact, he had often joined in when the missiles were thrown! So, weeks in advance, he was already aware of what he would be expected to endure on the day, as well as the hours of effort he would have to spend afterwards getting himself properly clean again. There was no avoiding it! No hiding away! For several nights before, he couldn't sleep. All he could think of was the terrible ordeal awaiting him. Bearing in mind some of the awful things that would be thrown at him, I wouldn't have blamed Brian if he had harboured any last-minute thoughts about remaining a bachelor, if only to avoid the embarrassment and mess. He endured it happily, however, because he was very much in love with his soon-to-be bride.

Be honest now! What were your first thoughts when I described the messy ingredients which were poured all over Brian? I'm sure that, like me, you shuddered and uttered a loud and long 'Yeuck!' Then, as you began to picture the terrible mess, you began to feel dirty and uncomfortable until the whole idea disgusted you. Right?

Now try to imagine a little of how Jesus must have felt that night in the garden of Gethsemane only hours before his terrible ordeal. He was aware even then of all that was about to be 'thrown' at him. The awful ache of rejection because someone he had trusted was about to betray him for the price of a slave. His arrest and the indignity of the so-called courts of justice. The embarrassment and frustration of having to listen to all the lies they would tell about him. Then being stripped, viciously beaten and having to kneel while the hairs of his beard were ripped out one by one. The pain of the crown of thorns as it was thrust mockingly upon his head. The overwhelming rejection of the very people he had come to save: 'We don't want him! We want Barabbas! Take him away and crucify him!' The sadness of hearing Peter deny him so vehemently. The loneliness because most of his disciples would abandon him in fear. The humiliation and shame of being executed as a common criminal on a Roman cross. And, finally, the absolute agony of a long, long, excruciating death. Such knowledge would be enough to cause the most courageous among us to shudder:

He [Jesus] withdrew about a stone's throw beyond them [the disciples], knelt down and prayed, 'Father, if you are willing, take this cup from me; yet not my will, but yours be done.' An angel from heaven appeared to him and strengthened him. And being in anguish, he prayed more earnestly, and his sweat was like drops of blood falling to the ground.

(Luke 22:41–44)

Here Luke reveals a medical detail not given by Matthew or Mark in their accounts: 'his sweat was like drops of blood', something that only happens to people in extreme anxiety and distress. The ordeal confronting Jesus seemed so terrible to him, not even the presence of an angel coming directly from his Father was enough to ease his troubled soul.

After much deliberation and prayer, I do not believe that it was the thought of any physical suffering, awful though it would be, which caused Jesus such tribulation in Gethsemane that night. What he struggled with, I feel sure, was the repulsiveness of the horrible, uncomfortable, dirty, disgusting 'mess' which was about to be 'poured' on him spiritually as he hung on the cross. Only this time it would not consist of sugar and syrup, etc, but the 'mess' of all our sin:

> ... and the Lord has laid on him
> the iniquity of us all.

(Isaiah 53:6)

The stench and vileness of our 'filthy (literally 'pus-ridden') rags' (Isaiah 64:6) were to be borne by the one who knows no sin, who has been always clean and perfectly pure. And our mess is worse than the worst mess which could ever be poured over any soon-to-be bridegroom.

Think of the worst thing you have ever done wrong in your life, something you are too embarrassed or afraid to share with even your closest friend. Think how badly you felt when you had done it, how you struggled with its awful guilt and blame. Now multiply that one sin by a zillion, billion, million – and even that can't begin to touch the surface of all Jesus laid upon his shoulders that day, when he bore the sins of the world, the sins of every person in every generation since the creation of the universe.

How often we remember the terrible pain which wracked his physical body and forget the agony endured in his spirit and soul. Then, at the time when he needed most the love and support of his own Father, God turned his back on him, because, in his absolute righteousness, he cannot look upon sin. The Father who had always been there for him, was silent as he cried out on the cross.

Jesus was well aware that all of this was going to be thrown at him and this is why he wrestled so much in prayer in Gethsemane. He could have changed his mind. He could have refused to go through with it and simply walked away, but he didn't! He loves us too much to have abandoned us to Satan, too much to have given up on us.

I asked Brian if the ordeal he experienced before his wedding was worth all the embarrassment and effort. Looking me in the eye, he grinned and said, 'You bet it was worth it! Just to see Gillian walking up the aisle towards me, looking like a princess, was more than worth it. I'll never forget how she looked. All I could think was, *Thank God she's mine!*

One day it will be the same for Jesus, our heavenly Bridegroom. On that day, he will return for you and me as his much-loved Bride. Then we will be absolutely pure and spotless, a perfect reflection of his own beauty and glory. And he will be able to declare about us, 'Yes, it was certainly worth it. Thank you Father that they are all mine!'

How will our hearts respond on that wonderful day? I know what mine will say! 'Hallelujah, what a Saviour!'

Focus

Spend a few moments considering Jesus' amazing love which compelled him to take your sin to the cross.

Now respond with heartfelt thanksgiving and praise. Promise him you will confess your sins daily, to receive his forgiveness and cleansing.

Feed

Read Isaiah 61:10 and Isaiah 62:1–5.

Here Isaiah prophesies concerning the relationship between God and his chosen nation, Israel, represented by her capital city, Jerusalem. This side of Calvary, the prophecy also describes the relationship between Jesus and those he has redeemed (the 'new Israel'). In these verses, we have painted a vivid picture of the Lord as Bridegroom and the church as the much-loved Bride for whom, one day, he will return.

- How are the characteristics and appearance of the Bride described (61:10; 62:1–2)? Describe her beauty (62:3).
- What is the Lord's response to his Bride (62:4–5)?

NB   The name Beulah, translated 'married', has the sense of 'belonging to' and 'being protected' by God, as a husband commits himself to and cares for his wife.

In Eastern culture, a bride would spend hours bathing herself in oils, dressing and adorning herself with jewels in preparation for her bridegroom's arrival.

- Are there areas of your life which still require attention and cleansing, so that you are as beautiful a Bride as you can be for the Lord?
- Could any part of your life still be described as 'deserted' or 'desolate' (62:4)? Surrender it to the Holy Spirit for the Lord's healing touch, so that it can bear fruit from now on.

5

FORGIVENESS – GOD'S GIFT

Life as a lay-worker is anything but boring, especially in the realms of 'tentmaking'! Before any of you have visions of me swathed in metres and metres of canvas and sewing yarn, I am referring to the occasional secular employment I find myself taking on to supplement my support as a Christian worker (see Acts 18:2–3). The phrase about 'variety being the spice of life' comes to mind when I remember some of the temporary jobs I have taken on in the past. The most colourful and amusing has to be when I worked in Santa's Grotto in a large department store in Edinburgh one Christmas. (Honestly, the things some people will do just to pay the mortgage every month!) And let me tell you that very often it was the parents who were the most excited about seeing Santa!

A less colourful but more serious occupation, however, found me working for a while as a civil servant in – you'll need a deep breath for this one – the Office of the President of Social Security Appeal Tribunals, or OPSSAT for short. Suitably impressed? I hope so! This involved setting up tribunals for disabled people who were seeking compensation for injuries such as vaccine damage, occupational deafness, and so on. You can imagine that during my time there the one word which was used more than any other was the word 'compensation', ie 'payment due for injury inflicted'. It is a word used often in the media these days. A tabloid newspaper – let's call it 'The Daily I T L Lies' – prints slanderous things about 'Mr Saul True-Anyway'. And Mr S T-A, as the injured party, sues the newspaper and receives loadsadosh as compensation, ie 'payment due for injury inflicted'!

Have you ever had to pay compensation to someone? I would reckon that most, if not all of us, will have paid it at some time in our lives, because compensation doesn't involve only huge court cases and extortionate sums of money. It can be owed for less spectacular things

too. Compensation involves any case where injury (whether physical, mental, emotional or spiritual) is inflicted on an innocent party.

Let me give you a 'real-life' example from my childhood. When I was ten or eleven years old, I had to polish the shoes of every member of my immediate family (and there were six of us!) for a whole week (that's twelve shoes every evening for seven days, which is a lot of 'elbow-grease') just because I happened (inadvertently, of course) to tell a nosy neighbour to 'mind her own business!' ('payment due for injury inflicted'). I hasten to add that the neighbour was extremely nosy, and all I had done was to say to her face what some adults had been wanting to say to her for weeks but hadn't dared! I dared, and compensation was duly paid along with a very reluctant apology.

I can give you many such instances when I was forced to hand over my meagre pocket money to make amends for offences such as breaking windows, tearing clothes while climbing trees, and so on. However, I can also give examples when I was the 'innocent party' instead of the 'offender'. And how sweet it was to watch others having to pay for the injury they had inflicted upon me! One of my sisters once borrowed something of mine, without permission, and damaged it. What a delight it was to see her hand over some of her birthday money to pay for it. I didn't even like what she had broken, but it was the principle that mattered. I am ashamed to admit that it was a case of 'I'm owed compensation and I'm bloomin' well going to have it, even if it takes her a lifetime to pay!'

I am sure you can remember times when you were the innocent party and compensation was due to you for injuries inflicted by others – perhaps more recently than childhood. Be honest now! What would have happened if someone had asked you to give up the right to compensation, to waive the right to payment owed you for some offence or hurt? What would you have said? Giving up our rights to whatever we are genuinely entitled doesn't come easily, does it? It goes totally against our basic human nature.

However, all of us know someone who did give up the right to compensation, someone who very willingly waived the right to payment owed for injuries inflicted on him – injuries and offences so great that all the languages in all the world could never express adequately the vast amount of compensation owed. I'm referring to God himself, of course! Every time one of his laws is broken, every time one of his created human beings ignores him or wilfully turns their back on him, yet another injury is inflicted upon the Lord. That's a tremendous amount of injury and compensation accruing, so much that you and I could never repay it on our own. However, the Bible tells us that instead of demanding his rights and insisting that we pay what is due, God willingly gives up his right to compensation from us because of our faith in Christ's sacrifice at Calvary. OK, so the Bible may not use those exact words. It tells us instead that God *forgives*.

To God, forgiveness is more than just an idea or a 'blessed thought': it is a positive action, a deliberate act of the mind, emotion and will; something that takes sheer guts, determination and courage. In his earthly ministry, Jesus both preached forgiveness (see Luke 15:11–31) and practised it. Many times as he healed the sick and demonised, he was heard to say, 'Your sins are forgiven' (see Mark 2:1–12). Even in the agony of his final hours on the cross he was heard to express forgiveness, first for those who had nailed him there (Luke 23:34) and then to the dying thief at his side (Luke 23:39–43). In 1 John 1:8–9, a similar promise is extended to you and me:

> If we claim to be without sin, we deceive ourselves and
> the truth is not in us. If we confess our sins, he is faithful
> and just and will forgive us our sins and purify us from
> all unrighteousness.

Forgiveness is certainly a wonderful gift from God. Notice, however, that it is a gift which is meant to be shared. As well as God expressing forgiveness to us, he also expects the same from us, as his children. We are expected to express forgiveness to others. We are expected to waive all rights to compensation from those who have hurt or offended us – even if we are genuinely owed it!

Forgiveness is essential both in our relationship with God and in our relationship with each other. In fact, God has made one dependent on the other. This is seen in how Jesus taught his disciples to pray:

> 'Forgive us our debts,
>   as we also have forgiven our debtors...
> For if you forgive men when they sin against you, your
> heavenly Father will also forgive you. But if you do not
> forgive men their sins, your heavenly Father will not for-
> give your sins.'
>
> *(Matthew 6:12,14–15)*

In other words, we cannot be blessed each day with God's gift of for-giveness until we ourselves have given that same blessing to those who have wronged us. This means actively forgiving everyone who has ever offended us, whether or not they realise what they have done and whether or not they even want our forgiveness in the first place. 'A tall order!' you might say, and you'd be right. It isn't, however, impossible.

I know from my own experience what it is to be deeply hurt by those who claimed to care for me. The deeper and more painful the injury, the more difficult it is to want to forgive. I know, too, what it is to use anger as a means of numbing the ache we feel inside, to wear unforgiveness as a kind of emotional 'chain mail' to protect the heart from further hurt. However, in this particular instance, I took my wounded soul to Jesus, to receive comfort and healing from him. What's more, he understood exactly how I was feeling because he too has suffered in the same way.

After my hurts and fear had been healed, however, the Holy Spirit impressed strongly upon my heart that it was now time to forgive those who had wronged me. At first I tried to ignore him, confident that if he just looked at things from my point of view and saw the injustice of it all, he would allow me to hold on to the odd grudge or two. Needless to say, he didn't agree! Instead, he spoke to me powerfully through the parable of the unmerciful servant (Matthew 18:21–35). As a result, I made a list of everything in my life for which I had already been forgiven by God – a mammoth task which took me a long time. (In fact, had I not accepted quickly what the Lord was saying, I would still be writing that list now! I daren't even think what I might need forgiveness for in the years ahead!) Looking at it, I could do nothing but admit that the debt which God has already cancelled in my life is enormous, much bigger than I could ever repay. Is there any sin of mine which God has refused, or will refuse, to forgive? My answer, based on his word, has to be 'No! Praise his name!' Then why is it so hard to cancel the debts owed me by others?

With the Spirit's help, I was able then to approach the Lord and say, 'I'm sorry that my unforgiveness towards these people offends you. I can't forgive them on my own, Lord, but I do want to forgive. Help me, please, in the name of Jesus.'

God must have seen, in my heart, my sincere desire (no matter how small) to be rid of my grudges. Over the next few months, he released slowly all that was needed to turn my willingness into reality. I can honestly say that I no longer feel the same towards those who had hurt me; I no longer harbour a desire to hurt them in return. I have to confess that all the Holy Spirit had to work with was a 'mustard seed' amount of willingness on my part. This is all I could offer in sincerity at the time. But he took it, nurtured it in my heart and mind, and helped it to grow, until finally I could surrender my anger and take off my 'armour' of unforgiveness.

'I tell you the truth, if you have faith as small as a mustard seed, you can say to this mountain, "Move from here to there" and it will move. Nothing will be impossible for you.'

(Matthew 17:21)

I am aware that Jesus is speaking here about faith. But if such a tiny amount of faith can work the miraculous, surely a similarly small amount of sincere willingness can be used to remove the emotional 'mountains' which hold us back?

'Nothing will be impossible for you.' That's God's promise!

Focus
Close your eyes and picture yourself laden with packages of all different shapes and sizes. Each package represents a grudge you bear against those who have wronged you in the past.

Now picture the Lord holding out a large, brightly coloured gift to you. Inside is his forgiveness which he wants you to receive. Your arms are full of packages and you cannot take it from him. What must you do now to be able to accept God's gift?

Lay down each package (or grudge) by praying in this way:

Lord, I want to forgive *(person's name)* for *(the injury inflicted)*. I release them unreservedly, in the name of Jesus. Please take my willingness and make it a reality, for your glory. Amen.

When you have done this sincerely, picture yourself reaching out and accepting God's gift of forgiveness to you.

Feed
Stephen has been chosen by the disciples to undertake some of the practical tasks within the New Testament church.

Read Acts 6:1 – 8:1.
- Define the emotions which motivated the Jews to pick up stones against Stephen (6:8–10,15; 7:54).
- Describe fully the ways in which Stephen was wronged (6:11–14; 7:57–60).
- What motivated Stephen's response in 7:60 (6:5,8; 7:55–56)?
- Who helps us to forgive (6:5; 7:55)?

Read John 8:1–11.

- What (besides Old Testament law, see Leviticus 20:10) catalysed the Pharisees' desire to pick up stones against the woman (v 6)?
- How had the woman 'offended' the Lord (vs 3–5)?
- What do you think motivated Jesus' response (v 11)?

What do these two incidents teach you to do next time you are tempted to 'pick up stones' against someone you believe has wronged you? Pray now that the Holy Spirit will help you in this.

6

IN HIS ARMS OF LOVE

One of the most personal and intimate pictures found in scripture of our relationship with God is that of God as heavenly Father and we as his spiritual children. There are many references to how God the Father loves us, provides for us, watches over us and desires the very best for our lives.

My favourite verses, however, are in the book of Hosea.

'When Israel was a child, I loved him,
and out of Egypt I called my son.'

(11:1)

'It was I who taught Ephraim to walk,
taking them up in my arms;
but they did not know that
it was I who healed them.'

(11:3, Amplified Bible)

'I led them with cords of human kindness,
with ties of love;
I lifted the yoke from their neck
and bent down to feed them.'

(11:4)

The picture of Father God holding his children in his arms is a very powerful one. Why?

Let me ask those of you who are mothers, what was the first thing you wanted to do immediately after giving birth to your child? Did you tell the midwife to stick your new baby in a cot by the side of your bed until you had enjoyed a cup of tea and a snooze? Of course not!

The first thing you wanted to do, I'm sure, was to gather your child in your arms and hold them. You wanted to feel the warmth of their tiny body against your own, to feel the tiny heart beating next to yours. You wanted to know immediately that all was well with them. You wanted personal contact. Why? Just because your baby was yours, and you wanted them to sense somehow by your touch that they were loved and accepted. You wanted your baby to feel secure as you held them in your arms.

God our Father is no exception: 'I took them up in my arms,' he says. In scripture, his arms are a symbol of safe refuge as he gently loves and protects his children. They are strong and mighty, able to support, deliver and conquer – for ever! They never lose strength and grow weary as ours do, especially after carrying a toddler around the house for a while!

> 'The eternal God is your refuge,
>   and underneath are the everlasting arms...'
>
> *(Deuteronomy 33:27)*

Being single, I have no children of my own, but I do know what it is for my friend's little boy, Joseph, to fall asleep in my arms, and for me to have to carry him upstairs to bed. I know that it's almost impossible to carry a sleeping child at arm's length. Contact has to be close, close enough to feel the warmth of his breath on my cheek. This is how close God wants his relationship with his children to be. He cannot love us, protect us and carry us through difficulties by keeping us at a distance.

So how should we, his children, respond to his arms around us? Well, how do small children react when they are picked up and carried? Do they panic and try to grab at some other means of support, just in case they are dropped? Of course not! I am sure that they would feel secure enough to relax and rest in their parent's arms. If you are a parent, I think you would be deeply hurt if your child grabbed frantically at other means of support whenever you held them: that would communicate to you that they really didn't trust you not to drop or harm them.

The same happens in our relationship with Father God. As his children, we should be living and behaving in a way that shows we feel secure in his keeping and trust him completely to 'carry' us. When we experience this deep security and trust in him, we will no longer want to waste valuable time and energy grasping at other 'means of support': we will stop looking to things like money, property, position, success, popularity, or any of the world's other status symbols, to help us feel significant and safe. Now I am not saying that our heavenly Father never means us to have these. What I am saying is that the more we grow in him, the less desire we will have to make them our ultimate priorities in life. All that will be important is our personal and intimate relationship with the Lord. Sensing those all-powerful yet gentle arms around us, we will be able to declare time and time again, like the apostle Paul, 'For to me, to live is Christ and to die is gain' (Philippians 1:21).

Focus

Close your eyes and picture yourself in the arms of God. See how firmly he holds you and shelters you.

Now examine your life and confess those things that have become 'props' to help you feel secure and significant. Ask the Holy Spirit to enable you to trust God more and to rely less on human 'supports'.

Feed

Read Philippians 3:2–10.

If anyone had reason to be self-confident and proud, it was the apostle Paul, in the light of his illustrious and zealous background. Yet he had been happy to sacrifice everything in order to know Christ in a personal and spiritually intimate way.

- Before his conversion, in what ways had Paul 'put confidence in the flesh'? How did these change when he came to faith in Christ?
- In what ways did you 'place confidence in the flesh' before you were a Christian? Where is your confidence placed now?

Read Philippians 4:10–13.
- How does Paul's personal relationship with Christ make a difference in his attitude to circumstances?
- Can you make the same declaration in your own personal relationship with Christ?

7

HIDING PLACE

Of the many people present in my life as I was growing up, one who held a great deal of positive influence over me was my grandmother on my mother's side of the family. We called her 'Grannie', and what a character she was! Standing no more than one and a half metres high, she looked delicate and fragile – but, let me tell you, she had a spirit of iron and a heart of pure gold! How fondly I remember her. Whenever she felt unable to manage a smile, we were never disappointed because there would always be a cheerful song on her lips instead. We regarded her as the fount of all knowledge, since she could always be relied upon to give sound advice on even the most obscure subjects. She was lively and humorous, brightening up, always, the dullest of days.

If asked what I remember most about Grannie, I would have to mention the colourful floral aprons she would wear each day. These were what were known fashionably as 'cross-overs', the idea being that once she had placed her arms through the armholes, she would then ensure that the flaps at the front were crossed over each other, before tying their strings behind her. Well, that was what was meant to happen! The problem was that my grannie rarely tied them. For reasons best known to herself, she preferred to have the flaps hanging loosely in front of her. Admittedly, she looked a bit odd!

However, almost forty years later, I must confess that I will always be grateful for those dangling apron flaps, because they were used many times to bring comfort to a little girl's aching heart. Whenever I was distressed – whether I had fallen over, had an argument with one of my sisters or just had a rotten day at school – my grannie would notice my tears and, in her own gentle manner, would smile and say, 'Oh, Jeanette, my hinnie! Come away and coorie in! (Come and have a hug!) Come and have a wee bit o'love. You look as if you need it!'

Then, holding the flaps of her apron, she would open out her arms to me, inviting me to approach her for comfort. Without another word, I would run to her, throw my arms around her tiny waist and bury my face in her as I wept buckets. She would then cover me gently with her apron flaps, like a mother hen protecting her little chick with her wings. As I hid there beneath the folds of the cloth, she would talk to me softly, soothing me, encouraging me, assuring me that all would be well soon, while I sniffed and sobbed until all the anger, pain and frustration had left me. To this day, I remember her gentle warmth, the lovely mixture of smells which clung to her apron – the smell of newly made broth or the distinctive smell of the household soap she used when scrubbing the floors – both familiar and very comforting. I could have stayed quite happily in this hiding place forever! My grannie, however, had other ideas. In her wisdom, she allowed me to remain hidden for no more than a few minutes, until my initial distress was gone. Then, telling me to 'go and sort it out', she would open up the flaps again, make me blow my nose on her clean handkerchief and send me on my way much more peaceful than before.

Grannie died a few weeks before my sixteenth birthday, and for many months afterwards I missed my much loved hiding place. Imagine my sheer delight, therefore, when I became a Christian and discovered that I now have a divine hiding place, where I can go whenever I need comfort and encouragement.

> Therefore let everyone who is godly pray to you
>   while you may be found;
> surely when the mighty waters rise,
>   they will not reach him.
> You are my hiding place;
>   you will protect me from trouble
>   and surround me with songs of deliverance.
>
> *(Psalm 32:6–7)*

The Almighty God himself is now my hiding place and I can run to him at any time, whenever danger, pain, sickness, embarrassment, temptation, lack of confidence or any other spiritual attack comes against me. Like my grannie all those years ago, he now covers me, only not with any apron flaps but with his mighty wings.

> Surely he will save you from the fowler's snare
>   and from the deadly pestilence.
> He will cover you with feathers,

and under his wings you will find refuge;
his faithfulness will be your shield and rampart.

(Psalm 91:3–4)

Many times in my Christian life have I hidden beneath the covering of those wings and wept many tears. On every occasion I have been comforted by the warmth of his presence, the tenderness of his love and the beautiful fragrance of Jesus, his Son.

I want to encourage you today that whenever you are distressed, under attack from the fiery arrows of the evil one or just finding life in general a little too much to handle, then run into the shelter of those mighty wings of God. They are already held wide open for you, inviting you to go in and receive whatever comfort your heart longs for at this time. Go on. Enter in and enjoy!

Focus

Invite the Holy Spirit to give you a picture in your mind of those mighty wings of God. Close your eyes and imagine yourself being covered by them, until you are completely hidden.

Now tell the Lord all that is troubling you today. Wait quietly while, by his Holy Spirit, he binds up your heart and comforts you.

Thank the Lord for his love, his care and his divine protection.

Feed

The prophet Elijah lived and served God during the reign of King Ahab and his wife, Jezebel, who worshipped false gods. Jezebel's hatred of Jehovah and his servants made Elijah's work both difficult and dangerous.

Read 1 Kings 17:1–6.

* Whose idea was it for Elijah to escape to this hiding place for a while?
* How does God express his love and care towards Elijah?

Elijah goes on to win a great moral victory on Mount Carmel over the prophets of Baal (1 Kings 18). He probably supposed that Ahab, Jezebel and the rest of the nation would turn back to Jehovah as a result. Jezebel, however, had other ideas!

Read 1 Kings 19:1–16.

* Whose idea was it for Elijah to hide this time?
* Does God understand? How do we know (vs 5–7)?
* How do you think Elijah would be feeling at this time (vs 3–4)?

- After guiding him to the cave on Mount Horeb (vs 8–9), how does God comfort, teach and restore Elijah? How does he comfort and restore you when you 'hide away' with him?
- Does the Lord allow Elijah to stay in hiding for long (vs 15–16)? What does he do instead? What do you think the Lord would say to you?

8

THE RAIN OF HARD TIMES

Have you noticed that television adverts for summer holidays seem to invade our screens earlier and earlier these days? No sooner have we packed away our suntan lotion after one year's vacation, than we are being tempted to book the following year's (only to take advantage of the unbelievable 'early bird' discounts, of course!) The blue-skied, sun-kissed locations currently on offer in the breaks between my favourite television programmes remind me of the holiday my friend Jenny and I enjoyed two years ago. It wasn't anything fancier than a 'cheap but cheerful' camping trip to Portugal, but it stays in my mind because on our travels I saw something which made a deep impression on me.

On the outward journey, travelling through France, we drove alongside a huge field of sunflowers, and if you have ever seen acres and acres of golden sunflowers, you will know how impressive a sight it can be. I was very inspired by what I saw. Hundreds of thousands of tall proud plants, the majority of them standing taller than myself, heads raised majestically towards the brilliant sun, petals bright and glimmering in the sunlight. How strong and invincible they looked!

Little did I know it then, but I was in for a real surprise (a shock even!) on the return journey. On the way home several weeks later, we passed the same field with exactly the same crop of sunflowers in it. But what a change had taken place! Instead of rows and rows of strong, upright, healthy-looking plants, I now saw flowers that were bedraggled and limp. Heads that had once been held high were now drooping and miserable. The same stalks that had stood majestic and tall were now bent double.

What had brought about such a dramatic change in those sunflowers? Very simply, the weather had altered! Gone was the gloriously warm sunshine in which I had first seen them basking. Now a fierce thunderstorm raged all around them. This whole field of sunflowers was being pelted mercilessly by heavy rain, and they were struggling to cope. The pressure of the raindrops on their delicate heads had them lying almost face down on the ground.

Very gently, the Holy Spirit showed me how those sunflowers were a picture of myself and how I am at times in my life as a Christian. Mostly, I am rejoicing, face turned towards the Lord, basking, if you like, in the 'sunshine' of the Father's goodness and blessing. When things are going well for me, I stand strong and spiritually 'tall'. Sadly, however, from time to time, the 'weather' changes. Dark 'clouds of trouble' seem to cover the 'sun'. The 'rain of hard times' comes pelting down on me, and I become 'bowed down' and miserable. It becomes a real struggle to 'keep my head up' until the storm passes and I can bask again in spiritual 'sunshine'.

Much as I'd like to, I cannot pretend that the Lord never allows this 'rain of hard times' to fall on his children. He certainly does! And when the rain comes, he doesn't always step in to give us shelter. In my own life over the years, the 'rain' has appeared in the form of difficult circumstances, sickness, weariness, financial worries, problems in relationships, and so on. I remain convinced, though, that God, our loving and perfect heavenly Father, never allows these to happen without a good and very necessary reason (although it may not seem like it at the time). He isn't a terrible ogre wanting only to spoil things for us, as I have often heard non-Christians declare.

If God loves us and wants only the best for us, why then does he permit the rain of hard times to fall? Surely we need our attention focused fully on the things he has asked us to do, without negative 'diversions' cropping up? Why then doesn't the Lord shield us from trouble so that we can give all our energy and best efforts to witnessing and winning souls for his kingdom? The simplest answer, I believe, is that the Lord allows hard times to come, because he has much to teach us in them and through them, lessons we could never learn in the sunshine of his goodness and blessing.

In her song entitled 'Hard Times', Jamie Owens writes:*

Is the rain falling from the sky keeping you from singing?
Is that tear falling from your eye because the wind is
stinging?
Don't you fret now, child. Don't you worry.
The rain's to help you grow –
So, don't try to hurry the storm along.
The hard times make you strong!

A question I have often asked the Lord is, 'How do hard times help us to grow?' Understanding even a little of why we suffer in our lives may help us to endure them more easily. Through my reading of scripture over the past months, I have come to realise, first of all, that hard times teach us true humility and total dependence on God.

> All men are like grass,
>   and all their glory is like the flowers of the field.
> The grass withers and the flowers fall,
>   because the breath of the Lord blows on them.
>
> *(Isaiah 40:6–7)*

The Father often allows the rain of hard times to soak us in order to help us keep things in perspective, spiritually; to remind us that on our own we are feeble and frail, that apart from God we can do nothing (John 15:5). The struggle we experience during hard times causes us to remember just how weak and helpless we really are as humans, and to realise how much we need God's power in our lives.

Another reason why God allows the rain of hard times to fall is to test our faith in him. Peter confirms this in his first letter:

> In this you greatly rejoice, though now for a little while
> you may have had to suffer grief in all kinds of trials.
> These have come so that your faith – of greater worth
> than gold, which perishes even though refined by fire –
> may be proved genuine and may result in praise, glory
> and honour when Jesus Christ is revealed.
>
> *(1 Peter 1:6–7)*

Hard times are allowed into our lives so that we can prove again what a powerful God we belong to! Through them we learn also how to persevere in spiritual battle as the Holy Spirit trains us in how to wield the spiritual weapons of scripture, prayer and praise (Ephesians 6:10–18). Experiencing hard times teaches us that God's promises are absolutely reliable. Applying them to our lives in faith is like holding up a spiritual umbrella under which to shelter. I have come to realise how positively the rain of hard times can unite the Body of Christ, as Christians join together and stand shoulder to shoulder against our common enemy, the devil.

Lastly, hard times come often simply to speed up the usual spiritual maturing processes which might otherwise take a long time to work in us. We learn obedience much more quickly by being allowed to suffer the negative consequences of our disobedience than by merely listening to a warning in a lecture or sermon. I can vouch for that!

As a child I used to ride my two-wheeler bike using the 'Look, no hands!' method. Although I couldn't do it nowadays, I was pretty good at it then. My mother warned me over and over again what would happen if I insisted on doing this, but as usual I paid little attention. One day, however, I was riding along quite happily, hands folded across my chest. I didn't notice some broken glass on the road. As I rode over it, my front tyre went 'Bang!' I went flying over the handlebars, landing in a heap in my neighbour's garden. My pride and a few other things were hurt that day, and I never ever took my hands off the handlebars again when I cycled. A lesson my mother had tried for months to teach me was learned in thirty seconds flat!

When you do find yourself struggling with hard times, never forget that God is in them with you. That's his promise: 'When you pass through the waters, I will be with you' (Isaiah 43:2). The Lord is always in complete control. He knows exactly what he is doing in our lives, as well as why he is doing it. Once we have learned all that he had planned to teach us in the rain, he will carry us out into sunshine again.

Let's picture once more that field of drooping sunflowers. It isn't surprising that they weren't able to cope with the thunder and rain: as their name suggests, they were made to live and grow only in hot climates, and for a short time only, before being harvested for their oil. You and I, however, are very different. As our name suggests, we are the children of God, brothers and sisters of Christ, with his very own Spirit, his very own character, his very own determination and power living within us. We are intended to become 'more than conquerors' (Romans 8:35–37), no longer the victims of our difficult circumstances but, rather, the victors over them!

Let me tell you about a beautiful yellow rose which stands in my parents' front garden in Scotland. It is a winter rose, blooming every year in time for Christmas. A few years ago, my parents' home was gutted by fire and that poor little flower had to contend with all kinds of hassle. First, a huge pane of glass from the sitting-room window collapsed on top of it. Then it endured litres and litres of water from the fire-fighters' hoses, as well as their great, heavy boots clomping all over it. Finally, all kinds of charred debris were tossed on it. Yet, in spite of everything it suffered, that beautiful rose is still there, standing healthy and strong. What's more, it will probably still be standing there next year and for several years to come, despite the wind, sleet and snow which Scotland is famous for! Why? Because as a winter rose it was created to endure, just like you and I. Praise God!

Is the rain falling from the sky keeping you from singing?
Is that tear falling from your eye because the wind is stinging?
Don't you fret now, child. Don't you worry.
The rain's to help you grow –
So, don't try to hurry the storm along.
The hard times make you strong!

Focus

Are you struggling with difficulties today? If so, present them to the Lord, inviting the Holy Spirit to show you what he wants you to learn from them. Ask the Lord Jesus for grace, patience and strength enough to endure, and for a teachable spirit.

If there are no difficulties in your life today, praise God! It may be that you are aware of others who are struggling. Pray for them.

Feed

Paul wrote his letter to the church in Philippi while he was under house arrest in Rome and chained twenty-four hours a day to a Roman guard. The purpose of his letter was to encourage the church and prepare them for the persecution which he knew was about to cause them great suffering and anguish.

Read Philippians 4:4–9.

Here Paul commands the Philippian Christians to rejoice even though they know that the rain of hard times is about to come pelting down on them. In these verses he gives pointers on how they can still achieve 'joy in all circumstances'. As you consider each one, note down, prayerfully, some practical ways in which you might make them work for you.

- 'Rejoice in the Lord always' (v 4).
- 'Let your gentleness be evident to all' (v 5).
- 'Do not be anxious about anything' (v 6).
- 'In everything, by prayer and petition, with thanksgiving, present your requests to God' (v 6).
- 'Whatever is true, whatever is noble, whatever is right, whatever is pure, whatever is lovely, whatever is admirable … think about such things' (v 8).
- 'Whatever you have learned or received or heard from me, or seen in me [or other Christians worthy of your respect] – put it into practice' (v 9).

And the God of peace will be with you.

Note

© Jamie Owens. Bud John Songs/Copycare.

9

OUR DIVINE BODYGUARD

'Well, it's finally happened!' I thought, rubbing my weary eyes. 'This African sun has finally broiled my brain!'

Yet I was convinced that I had just seen an armed guard parading past our bedroom window. I looked again. There was another and another! 'I think you'd better have a little lie down,' I told myself.

However, there was no mistake. There were indeed three very real khaki-clad soldiers, loaded rifles at the ready, patrolling outside our guest house.

The reason soon became obvious. A new guest had arrived – a very important high court judge who was about to pass judgement in a highly sensitive political case. His life was currently at risk, so he was guaranteed 'round the clock' protection. Well, that was supposed to be the plan! One evening, however, we arrived back at the guest-house after dark, when 'his Honour' had already gone to bed, and what did we find? Instead of being vigilant and active, all three soldiers were curled up asleep on the veranda. No one was on guard!

We woke them and asked, 'What are you doing here? You are supposed to be watching!' With a typically African shrug of the shoulders, they replied, 'It is the night. The night is for sleeping!' And on they snored until dawn.

The psalm I read that night reassured me:

> He [the Lord] will not let your foot slip –
>   he who watches over you will not slumber;
> indeed, he who watches over Israel
>   will neither slumber nor sleep.

> *(Psalm 121:3–4)*

Our divine Bodyguard is always alert and active, even in the middle of the night! He is always 'on the job', never needing to stop for a snooze. He works the night-shift as well as the day-shift, so his protection is one hundred per cent guaranteed. If I didn't believe that, I wouldn't even venture out of bed in the morning, far less travel half way around the world!

Psalm 121 goes on to make some other very positive statements of the truth:

> The Lord watches over you –
> the Lord is your shade at your right hand;
> the sun will not harm you by day,
> nor the moon by night.
> The Lord will keep you from all harm –
> he will watch over your life;
> the Lord will watch over your coming and going
> both now and for evermore.
>
> *(Psalm 121:5–8)*

Notice that it doesn't say that the Lord 'might', 'probably', 'if he feels like it', 'if there's an R in the month and the wind's blowing in the right direction' keep you from all harm. He will 'watch over your life'. No doubt or speculation. These statements are promises made by God through someone who had already claimed them and found them to be absolutely reliable in his own life and experience.

I am convinced that during our ministry trips to Tanzania, my co-worker Jenny and I have been exposed to dangers, some of which we were blissfully ignorant of at the time, especially in the spiritual realm. God, our protector, however – the one who sends us out in his very own name – knew about every one of them, and he acted on our behalf without us knowing what was happening. That is how vigilant he is.

Thousands of miles away, it was often difficult to contact friends and prayer partners back in the UK. There were few telephones, no 'mobiles' and a postal service which showed definite room for improvement, so often people had no idea what was happening to us there. But our divine Bodyguard knew. Every minute of every day, he knew where we were and how we were. In fact, he was right there with us. Our heavenly Father is the God who has his finger on the pulse of his children's lives. Whenever he sees danger ahead, or that we have a particular need, he moves in power to meet it.

Sometimes when I am greatly troubled and unable to sleep at night, the Lord whispers to me as I lie on my bed, 'I'm not sleeping either,

Jeanette!' And I remember Psalm 121. He then says, very gently, 'Why should we both be awake? Why don't you give me whatever is troubling you? I'll take care of you.' Then I close my eyes and again commit my way to the Lord (Psalm 37:5). In the Amplified Bible this verse is, 'Roll and repose each care of your load on him', and this is exactly what I do: I imagine myself rolling my burdens on to Jesus' shoulders and, before I know it, I'm at peace. Praise his lovely name!

Focus

Imagine your current worries as heavy burdens. See yourself taking them from your own shoulders and rolling them onto the Lord. Trust him to carry them for you and, once they have been surrendered, don't be tempted to take them back again.

Feed

Read Psalm 91.

This psalm is believed to have been written by David, using as background many of his real-life daring and dangerous exploits. Its theme highlights how God's people can live secure and blessed lives once they place themselves under God's almighty protection. Because David had actually experienced for himself the truths expressed here, the psalm has been written from the heart and not just from head-knowledge.

- What does David declare about God and about his own personal faith in him (vs 1–2)? From your own life and faith, can you make the same heart-felt declaration?
- Which promises are made in verses 3–13 ? What might be their modern-day equivalents?
- In verses 14–16, there are seven promises made by God to David. What are they? To some extent, those promises now apply to all Christians. Can you give personal testimony to their truth from your own daily experience, or from the experience of other believers?

10

'I'M A BIG GIRL NOW!'

Since my niece Nicola was almost four years old, she and I have often been up to mischief together. One of the things we loved to do was slide down the wooden banister in the hallway of my parents' home, despite frequent threats from my mother of what she would do if she ever caught us.

Nicola is now a teenager and, from the time she was nine or ten years old, I began to see a tremendous change in her each time I visited my family in Scotland. A few years ago a real surprise awaited me. On an afternoon when my mother was nowhere to be seen (or heard!), I whispered to Nicola, 'Shall we slide down Grannie's banister while she's not around to yell at us?' Quite unexpectedly, she drew herself to her full height (which even then was as tall as I am now), looked me directly in the eye and announced very politely, 'No, Auntie Jeanette! I don't do that any more. I'm a big girl now!' And off she went in search of a book to read.

You could have knocked me over with a feather! I realised then how quickly she was maturing, not just physically, but in her attitudes and her behaviour. Seemingly, no one has ever mentioned to her that she is too old to go sliding down banisters – she worked that one out all by herself. (Personally, I believe you're never too old!)

Then, at various times during my visit, she would surprise me by some of the statements she made: 'Girls my age don't play with Barbie dolls any more… Girls my age write diaries…' Or the one which, admittedly, made my eyebrows rise a centimetre or two when I heard it: 'Girls my age have lots of boyfriends'. Nowadays Nicola is deeply into designer-label sports gear (anything costing under £60 she won't even try on, never mind be seen wearing!) and she is a staunch Glasgow Rangers football fan. She is now at an age where she is realising, quite naturally, that how she behaved as a toddler may have been quite acceptable from a toddler, but is no longer acceptable now that she is growing into a lovely young lady. Although she would never express herself like this, what she is actually discovering about life is that natural maturity (growing up physically) brings with it the need to change in other areas, the need to grow up in the way she thinks, acts and speaks.

This is also the case with spiritual maturity, or 'growing up into Christ Jesus'. The apostle Paul teaches this in his letters to the new churches. To the church in Corinth, where immorality and spiritual indiscipline were rife, he writes:

> When I was a child, I talked like a child, I thought like a child, I reasoned like a child. When I became a man, I put childish ways behind me.
>
> *(1 Corinthians 13:11)*

In other words, the kind of behaviour that dominated our lives as unbelievers is no longer acceptable when we come to faith in Christ; so we must determine, with the Holy Spirit's help and encouragement, to set this behaviour aside.

In his letter to the church in Philippi, Paul describes this spiritual 'growing-up' process in terms of running a race.

> But one thing I do: Forgetting what is behind and straining towards what is ahead, I press on towards the goal to win the prize for which God has called me heavenwards in Christ Jesus.
>
> *(Philippians 3:13,14)*

What is the prize that awaits us at the finishing line? Spiritual perfection, complete wholeness in Christ.

A colleague, who is fit enough to run marathons, tells me that at regular stages of each race there are markers which indicate how far the competitors have come and how far they still have to go before they reach their goal, namely the finishing line. It is exactly the same in the spiritual race in which we Christians participate. At various stages along the way the Holy Spirit places pointers, or 'distance posts', which, when we become aware of them, encourage us to keep on going (or in this case 'growing'!) until we reach our goal in Christ.

What are the signs that tell us we are no longer 'baby Christians' but are growing spiritually? First, we will sense within us a deeper inner peace and trust in God. We will know assurance and a greater security in him. We will also sense a greater willingness to serve the Lord in obedient faith and to give to others as the Holy Spirit directs. We will come to know a greater willingness to love, to say sorry when we hurt others, and to forgive when others cause us pain. Above all, there will grow in us a sincere willingness to change in order to become like Jesus.

Nicola is certainly showing a desire to change as she grows up physically: 'I don't do that any more. I'm a teenager now!' She has begun to learn what is and what isn't suitable for a girl of her physical age and she is trying sincerely to make her behaviour match her years.

The word of God leaves us in no doubt that our attitudes and actions should be changing constantly to match our spiritual age if we are growing to full maturity as Christians. How the Lord will bless and encourage us each time we surprise our friends and family members when we declare gently but confidently, 'No! I don't do that any more. I'm a Christian now!'

Focus

Ask the Holy Spirit to show you what the Father considers still to be 'childish ways' in your spiritual life. When he does this, confess each one and ask him to help you set them aside.

Ask him to reveal to you the more mature qualities he now wants to create in you.

Thank the Lord for his patience and love.

Feed

Read Colossians 3:1–17.

In verses 5–14, Paul describes the 'earthly nature' (ie our old human nature) and the 'new self' (ie our renewed nature in Christ) in terms of garments which we either 'take off' or 'put on' (ie 'clothe ourselves with') when we become a Christian.

- What are the ungodly characteristics of the old earthly nature (vs 5–11)? Are any of these still present in your own life? Why can't they be allowed to remain there?
- What qualities should we be 'putting on' in their place (vs 12–14)? Name any which still need to be prayerfully and practically applied in your life.
- Name anyone you have difficulty 'bearing with' (v 13). Pray for them, asking the Lord to help you show more love and grace towards them.

11

DEAD FLIES STINK!

In Italy last summer I became involved in a new activity, an activity in which I participated every day for hours on end: the very necessary continental 'sport' of – wait for it – fly-swatting! And it wasn't by choice either! Never before in all our years of camping have there been so many flies. Overnight, our recently acquired plastic swat became a vital piece of equipment. It was never out of our sight. When we set the table for meal times, it was placed near at hand. It went to the beach with us and often came with me into the shower. That's how much of a nuisance the little blighters were. Though we didn't like doing it, we had to attack and destroy them. Why?

First, they constantly spoiled concentration. No matter what you were doing, they continually buzzed around, landing wherever they wanted. And the noise! When half-a-dozen of them congregated close to our ears, it sounded like Brand's Hatch on a busy race day! Then there were unbearable times when we were busy cooking or washing dirty clothes, and we didn't have a hand spare to brandish the swat. It was usually when every single fly in Europe (or so it seemed) suddenly descended on newly sunburnt arms, legs, necks and noses! Anybody watching from a distance and seeing my wild dance as I tried to shoo them away, would have thought I was crazy.

The things we found ourselves doing to cope with the problem! Much to my embarrassment, I began talking to the little blighters, threatening all kinds of terrible trouble if they didn't leave me alone: 'Just you wait! I'll get you! There's no place you can hide!' Eventually, we ended up making a game of it, to break the monotony. 'Get the fly' became a regular part of our daily routine. We devised a score system based on whether the fly was stationary or mobile when wellied, and there were double or treble points if you hit several at one swipe. And the skills we developed! Worthy of Wimbledon any day. The quick 'up and at 'em' forearm slam, the 'slow but steady' backhand lob, and so on – all were delivered with great zeal and panache.

Although I have made quite a joke of it so far, the main reason we destroyed those flies was a very serious one. The insects that came to tap-dance on top of our food and ourselves were also those which, only seconds before, had been scavenging in filthy rubbish bins and paddling in smelly drains. With all the germs they carried, they had the potential to incapacitate us physically and spoil the holiday.

Why am I rabbiting on about flies? Well, I am attempting to introduce a rather strange Bible verse which has fascinated me recently. It says this:

> As dead flies give perfume a bad smell, so a little folly
> outweighs wisdom and honour.
>
> *(Ecclesiastes 10:1)*

In Solomon's day, there were no cosmetics factories to churn out millions of litres of soaps and body lotions, so perfume would have been made by hand. The ingredients were a combination of fresh flower petals, exotic fruits and the bark of rare eastern trees, all carefully selected by the perfumer himself according to his own unique recipes. Then would follow a process of cleansing, crushing and pummelling, again by hand for hours on end, to release the natural scented juices. These were boiled at very high temperatures to purify the ointment and give it a smooth thick texture.

Because of the considerable time, care and effort involved, the end product would have been very precious and costly. Huge quantities of each ingredient were needed to make just a few grams of ointment, which again added to its tremendous cost. The ointment which Mary poured onto Jesus' feet would have cost more than a whole year's wages (Mark 14:5).

After cooling the mixture, the perfumer would carefully pour it into marble or alabaster flasks, into the necks of which he would place stone or metal stoppers. These were sealed with wax to protect what was by now an exotic and highly expensive substance, and to make sure that none of its delicious fragrance was wasted. These flasks of personal, precious and protected ointment were then made available to special customers at exorbitant prices. They were usually purchased by wealthy men as love gifts for the women in their lives (there being no such thing in those days as handmade Swiss chocolates!). The purpose of such substances was varied. The most highly scented were used

Dead flies stink!

for cosmetic purposes. Those made from herbal ingredients only were used medicinally to soothe and to heal. Others were used simply to bring coolness and comfort in the tremendous heat and dryness of the climate.

Have you realised yet that this ointment created by the perfumer is a picture of the new life Christians enjoy in knowing Jesus? It is a personal life, chosen and designed for us according to our Creator's own special 'recipe' and received by us through faith and repentance. Then it is a precious life, costing the exorbitant price only Jesus was able and willing to pay. He purchased it through his sacrifice on the cross and gave it to us freely to show how much he loves us.

> For you know that it was not with perishable things such
> as silver or gold that you were redeemed from the empty
> way of life handed down to you from your forefathers, but
> with the precious blood of Christ, a lamb without blemish
> or defect.
>
> *(1 Peter 1:18–19)*

It is also a pure life, cleansed by the blood of the Lamb: and that is how the Holy Spirit means to help us keep it – as fresh and untainted as the day it was given us. The more we seek to keep ourselves spiritually pure, the more effectively the Lord can use us in his kingdom.

> But thanks be to God, who always leads us in triumphal
> procession in Christ and through us spreads everywhere
> the fragrance of the knowledge of him. For we are to God
> the aroma of Christ among those who are being saved
> and those who are perishing.
>
> *(2 Corinthians 2:14–15)*

We can also describe it as a protected life because it is sealed by the Holy Spirit himself, who lives in us and shows us constantly how to walk in obedience to God. Because of our special covenant relationship with God, our heavenly Father has a responsibility to protect his children. The Bible is full of promises that he will do this.

The ointment referred to by Solomon in Ecclesiastes 10:1 would have started out as a pure and precious substance, but it became 'polluted' because it had been spoiled by the carcasses of dead scavengers. Imagine a scene we have all witnessed in the summer-time – an uncovered dish of melting butter into which several inquisitive flies have nose-dived and then drowned as a result. Not a pretty sight! In fact, it probably looked so ugly and uninviting, you have sworn never to eat butter again! In the same way, the perfumer's polluted ointment has become just as ugly and uninviting. You would be reluctant to touch it with the tip of your tiniest finger, never mind smearing it over your whole body. If the sight of it didn't put you off, the smell certainly would. Rotting fly carcasses would eventually cause the ointment to stink. Its once beautiful and exotic fragrance would be replaced in time by an obnoxious stench far worse than the smelliest socks you could ever imagine. Whew!

As well as becoming ugly and uninviting, the perfumer's ointment would also be rendered useless. Without its appealing fragrance, it could never again be used for cosmetic purposes. With its smooth and luxurious texture spoiled by ugly black lumps, the ointment could never again be used to cool and comfort the body. The fly carcasses, and all the germs they carry, have contaminated the ointment such that it can never again be used to soothe and heal. This once precious substance – whose creation involved so much time, attention and care – would now be completely ruined, good enough only to be buried or binned. What a waste!

Consider again the perfumer's original ointment as a picture of the pure and precious new life we receive through faith in Jesus. In Ecclesiastes 10:1 we seem to have a clear warning that if care is not taken, this too can become polluted in some way. I am sure we realise how displeased Satan was when we called on the Lord to deliver us from evil. Now he is even more unhappy because the 'aroma of Christ' within us draws others around us towards the kingdom of God. He is determined, therefore, to do all that he can to taint the image of Jesus within us. He wants to contaminate our witness so that it is no longer effective and fruitful. So he sends out his spiritual 'flies' to buzz all around us, to tempt, trouble and tease us, to spoil our concentration, to hinder our work for God, and to threaten our spiritual health and happiness.

These spiritual 'flies' are not necessarily demonic spirits. Most often, they are simply the negative, fearful and ungodly influences that swarm around us daily, in our places of work and leisure, on television, in many of the newspapers and magazines we allow into our homes, even in some of the people we rub shoulders with everyday.

Now, before you begin thinking that staying in bed all day is the only way to avoid these spiritual 'nasties', let's have a look at 1 John 4:4:

> You, dear children, are from God and have overcome
> them, because the one who is in you is greater than the
> one who is in the world.

Here we are assured that there is no reason to fear the devil or any of
the ungodly influences he sends to trouble us. Although they may
attack us, they can never overpower us as long as we heed the words
of James (4:7): 'Submit yourselves, then, to God. Resist the devil, and
he will flee from you'. As long as we walk daily in obedience to the
Lord, then victory is ours in Christ and God will fulfil his promise of
giving us daily protection.

At the beginning of every day, take time to submit yourself to God's
perfect will. Declare again your allegiance to his kingdom. Stand
under the banner of Christ, claiming the power of his shed blood to
protect you. Put on the full supernatural armour of God and take up
the spiritual weapons of scripture, prayer and praise. Declare again
your love for the Lord and your desire to walk more closely with him.
Ask for the Holy Spirit's help to stay clean spiritually. Give him permission to do whatever he needs to, so as to preserve the precious and
pure 'aroma of Christ' in you. Heed his voice as he warns you what and
whom to avoid each day.

Then get out there and wield the divine 'fly swat' he has given you.
Use it to squash any temptation and fear which attacks you. What is
this divine 'fly swat'? The all-powerful name of Jesus (Philippians
2:9–11)! Carry it with you wherever you go, using it as often as you
need to, and watch those nasty spiritual 'flies' scatter as you wield its
authority in faith!

> To him who is able to keep you from falling and to pre-
> sent you before his glorious presence without fault and
> with great joy – to the only God our Saviour be glory,
> majesty, power and authority, through Jesus Christ our
> Lord, before all ages, now and for evermore! Amen.
>
> *(Jude 24–25)*

Focus

Close your eyes and imagine that you are holding in your hands an
unpolluted jar of perfumer's ointment. If you find this difficult, invite
the Holy Spirit to help you. Imagine its wonderful aroma. If it were
real, what would you need to do to ensure that it never lost its purity
and freshness?

Imagine now your life in Christ. What practical measures do you need to take to make sure that your Christian walk and witness remain effective and fruitful? Determine in your heart that all ungodly compromise must go.

Feed

Read 1 Corinthians 10:13; Hebrews 2:18; 4:14–16; James 1:13–14.

What can you learn from these verses to help you cope when tempted?

12

BLUE BLOBS RULE! OK?

'Enemy aircraft overhead, sir! Permission to engage?'

'Permission granted,' came the reply, and off they charged – four chubby fourth years, fingers pointing to the sky, eyes half-closed against the glare of the sun. 'Ratatatat! Ratatatat!' they screamed at the top of their voices. Their 'target', a small light-weight plane conspicuously poised in the blue autumn sky, flitting in and out of tiny clusters of cloud.

From the Infant playground, infectious giggling could be heard. A group of first-year children, filled with excitement, were demonstrating how to use skipping ropes for everything except skipping. In childish minds, they had become wonderful playthings – reins for chariot horses that ride like the wind, cowboy lassoes for roping cattle, safety harnesses for intrepid mountaineers...

Suddenly a gruff voice bellowed above the others. A small, fair-haired 'cowboy' had accidentally fallen from his 'trusty stallion'. His pathetic sobbing suggested at least a broken limb, but expert examination revealed nothing more than one grazed elbow, two muddied hands and a suspected saddle-sore bottom!

Meanwhile, back on the Junior 'battlefield', the daily 'murder-by-football' match was underway. Anyone still standing at the final whistle was a 'softie'! All thirty-odd players (seventeen-a-side at the last count) thundered boisterously across the concrete pitch, making up the rules and arguing over them as they went along. Their faces were serious. Their eyes betrayed the fact that their minds were as active as their feet. Today a proud Priory player, tomorrow the World Cup!

Barely a metre away, brave netballers went through their paces.

'One ... two...'

'Aim ... throw...'

'Hard lines! Try again!'

Brows creased with concentration, would-be goal scorers balanced on tip-toe, like Russian ballerinas. Behind them, huddled in a corner, stood the 'nonconformists', blatantly united in their common vow never to exercise unless absolutely forced to! Far better to crowd in little clusters sharing stories, secrets, sayings, sadnesses...

'She never?'

'Really?'

'Oh, that stinks!'

'Hope she tells 'im what she thinks of 'im!'

Just then, a bright, blue Blob appeared on the horizon. Conspicuous amongst the red and grey school uniforms, this lone midday supervisor slipped stoically by. Rosy-cheeked, eyes darting here and there, mercilessly prodded and poked by youngsters desperate for attention, she made her way across the playground. The netballers hesitated nervously, mid-throw. Frustrated footballers moved aside, anxious for the intrusion to be over quickly.

Although affectionately known as 'Mrs Dinner Lady', the Blob was aware that her authority was absolute. As she approached a group of slipping infants, her mind philosophised: 'Never mind the National Lottery. Just give me a fiver for every time I've had to yell "Mind those wet leaves!" and I'll be richer than Rockerfeller!'

A clammy infant hand was slipped into hers, its distressed owner seeking comfort and encouragement. A bored 'mountaineer' came to tell her what Santa would bring him if he were good. The delicious odour of turkey curry and chips wafting from the kitchen reminded the Blob that she was as yet unfed. Her mouth began to water. She raised her free hand to look at her wrist-watch. 'Only one more minute to go!' She mentally counted the seconds...

The long awaited bell sounded from the inner sanctum of the staff room, rung by a reluctant Head. The shrill sound of the playground whistle was quickly drowned by the thudding of 170 pairs of feet. They lined up in classes, cowboys, footballers, charioteers alike, all fantasies, dreams, hopes for the future hastily wrapped and stored away in eager minds – at least until afternoon play! Thudding feet became marching feet, their rhythm interspersed with stifled giggles as a silly third year performed his daily 'trip-up' routine. Then – unadulterated silence!

For a moment, this had a profound effect on the Blob, as if some Higher Power had suddenly switched off the mighty Falls at Niagara, as if the great London Philharmonic had suddenly cut short its performance of Tchaikovsky's *1812* Overture. Peace, perfect peace, at last! Still, Blobs should never grumble. Where else would they be treated to such a feast of entertainment? Where else could they enjoy the drama of the theatre, the excitement of Wembley, the sensations of a circus, the over-emotionalism of TV soaps, and up-to-the-minute local gossip – and it not cost a penny? And there's much, much more to come – same time, same place – tomorrow!

If I were ever to write a book about my exploits as a senior midday supervisor in a local primary school (which is what a Christian friend so lovingly refers to as my 'other job'), it would probably be called 'Mrs Dinner Lady's Diary', and what you have just read would be a 'tongue-in-cheek' extract from it. I have led a team of dinner ladies for six years now, and I love it – because, if nothing else, it's far from boring! Every day there is something new to savour – new challenges, new choices and, yes, new crises, all of which we try to meet with compassion, care and a cheery grin. (Well, on good days at least!)

Now at the risk of sounding as if I've been promoted suddenly to divine status, I've come to notice over the months many similarities between some of the things I do as a dinner lady and the way in which the Holy Spirit works in the lives of God's children. OK, so you think this is a bit far fetched? Just bear with me a while and I'm sure I'll convince you!

Most of my time is spent walking around the dining room and playgrounds, watching and weighing up mentally whether what's going on there still ensures a safe environment for the children in my care. The presence of my fellow team members (or should I say, fellow Blobs) and myself gives each child a subconscious sense of security. They know immediately where to come when they are in trouble or needing help and advice. Isn't that exactly what the Holy Spirit's presence in our lives means to us?

During Jesus' last few hours with his disciples before his arrest and death, he told them this:

'I will ask the Father, and he will give you another
Counsellor to be with you for ever – the Spirit of truth.
The world cannot accept him, because it neither sees him
nor knows him. But you know him, for he lives with you
and will be in you.'

(John 14:16,17)

The Greek word translated here as 'Counsellor' literally means 'someone who is called alongside someone else to help them'. The Holy Spirit's closeness in and around us should give us a strong sense of security in Christ.

The main purpose of the Blob team's presence at lunch times is not just to deal with nasty incidents and accidents after the event, but to try to anticipate these and take appropriate steps to prevent them happening in the first place. If anyone does end up falling over or bumping heads with a fellow classmate (a common occurrence!), a Blue Blob is soon there offering First Aid, comforting words and a warm, soothing smile. Isn't that, in a sense, what the Holy Spirit does in the lives of God's children?

The team is there to offer friendship to the pupils in our care. We often find ourselves listening to elaborate stories about what happened on the way to the dentist, about who's coming round to whose house for tea and whether they should have burgers or fish fingers with their chips and baked beans. ('What do you think, Miss?') Sharing fun and laughter with the children means being treated to the current in-joke about twenty times a day, teasing them with humorous comments, and having our own legs pulled in return. And some of them are so brazen! Just before my 1996 visit to Africa, some of the children were quizzing me about whether or not it was safe to go. Someone asked, 'What will you do if a soldier points a loaded gun at you?' A very serious question, but that's the thing about the children in our school – they are never short of imagination! Before I had the chance to reply, one of the boys piped up,

'Don't worry, Miss! Just give 'em one of your 'looks'. That'll sort 'em!'

Then we are often asked for advice or to express an opinion on important matters: 'Who's going to win the FA cup this year, Miss?' 'What d'ya think of Posh Spice's new hairdo?' These may sound trivial to adult ears, but they are vitally important to trendy youngsters.

Often there are more scientific subjects discussed. Only yesterday I had to explain to a third year why there was steam rising from the playground after a heavy fall of rain. As I filled her in on the technical details (very simply, of course, because I only just understand them myself.), she gazed at me open-mouthed before saying, 'Oh, Miss! You're brilliant! You know everything!' I didn't reply. Well, you don't like to contradict young children, do you? It only confuses them!

Often I am asked about things of which I know nothing and I have to do some research at home before giving an answer the following day (my playground cred depends on it). Praise God that the Holy Spirit knows already the answer to any question I will ever ask him!

'All this I have spoken while still with you. But the Counsellor, the Holy Spirit, whom the Father will send in my name, will teach you all things and will remind you of everything I have said to you.'

(John 14:25,26)

'But when he, the Spirit of truth, comes, he will guide you into all truth. He will not speak on his own; he will speak only what he hears, and he will tell you what is yet to come.'

(John 16:13)

A large part of a Blob's time is spent acting as peacemaker when children disagree and fall out with each other. Getting an apology out of stubborn offenders is like drawing blood sometimes, but well worth it if it prevents blood being spilt! Of course, there are times when we have to rebuke children who continually abuse the rules which have been designed to keep them safe. If I had £1 (50p even!) for every time I've had to yell, 'Don't run down the stairs!', I'd be holidaying in the Bahamas this winter.

Then we often have to offer guidance to those in danger of wandering away from secure areas. It isn't the first time I have found myself having to sprint up the school driveway after a new infant when they decide they have had enough and want to go visit Grandma. Very gently and lovingly, I take them by the hand and patiently lead them back on to safe paths again. Isn't that what the Holy Spirit has to do from time to time in our lives?

Have I convinced you yet about the similarities between my job as dinner lady and what the Holy Spirit does in the lives of God's children? He offers us friendship and fellowship, comfort and healing, help and advice, guidance and teaching, rebuke when it is needed, and a safe environment in which to live and grow spiritually.

Perhaps, however, I should be more ready to admit the even greater similarities that exist between my behaviour as a child of God and that of the children in our school. I can be just as stubborn and wayward, just as mischievous and cunning, just as nosy and naive, just as reluctant to obey. Yet I know that the Holy Spirit is every bit as committed to me in my childlikeness of spirit as I am to the children in my care. He is always there for me as I try to be for them. He is committed to doing his very best in us and through us, for the glory of God and for our greatest good. His best is far, far better than mine will ever be. Praise God!

Focus

In what obvious ways has the Holy Spirit 'come alongside to help' you in your life as a Christian? Make a list and thank him for his involvement.

Identify the areas where you may still be a little hesitant or unwilling to allow him to become involved. Ask him to reveal the source of your reluctance and to help you overcome this, in the name of Jesus.

Feed

Jesus is on the Mount of Olives, teaching his disciples about his return to the earth 'at the end of the age' (Matthew 24:3). To help them understand more easily, he tells them a parable.

Read Matthew 25:1–13.

- Who does the character of the bridegroom represent?
- Who does the picture of the oil represent?
- How did the ten wise virgins ensure their lamps' maximum effectiveness for the bridegroom? How can you make sure that your Christian life and witness achieve maximum effectiveness for Jesus?

Read Luke 11:5–13.

- What still needs to be done in your life to guarantee your own readiness for the Bridegroom's return?

13

NEVER MIND THE GIANTS

'Never again will I complain about the state of British roads!' I vowed, as our beat-up old taxi struggled to transport us and our luggage high into the mountains of Tanzania. The huge dents which appear constantly in African roads make our potholes seem like pinholes. Honestly! Even the shortest of journeys leaves you feeling seasick.

An even greater ordeal, however, particularly for those with delicate stomachs, has to be walking from place to place. To begin with, I spent most of my time in Tanzania staring at the ground, being very careful where I placed my feet on the dusty roads. I could tell you in great detail about the dead rodents, the goats' excrement and all the other filthy rubbish that lay there, but don't ask me about the gorgeous sunsets or beautiful scenery. I couldn't have said much about those because my eyes were focused in the wrong direction and on the wrong things. However, as I was carried higher into the mountains in my taxi, I was challenged by the Old Testament story of Caleb.

Caleb and eleven others were sent out by Moses to spy out the land of Canaan before the Israelites moved in to take possession of it (Numbers 13–14). They too would have headed for the mountains, from where it was possible to survey the whole countryside without being seen. From the reports they brought back on their return to camp, we can imagine how those spies might have behaved on that patrol into unknown territory.

The majority of them, I think, would have been over-cautious, probably looking constantly over their shoulders or with their eyes glued to the ground, searching for booby traps. Just imagine them discovering the signs that revealed that there were giants living there: 'Whoa! Will you look at the size of those footprints! They're enormous! We'd better watch out!' Then, actually seeing for themselves those giant 'sons of Anak' (13:28,33). And all the time they were robbing themselves of everything that could, in fact, have encouraged them. They allowed their fear to determine the kind of report they would take back to Moses and the others.

Not Caleb, however! I can imagine him striding along calmly, confident that God, who had chosen them and then sent them out through Moses, was himself watching over them, keeping them safe. Instead of staring down at the ground, I can imagine him looking upwards and all around him, like a child in a toy shop, absolutely delighted by everything he saw, amazed by its richness and beauty. 'Look at that waterfall! Isn't it wonderful? Mmm, have you tasted this fruit? It's delicious!' I can imagine Caleb refusing to let fear rob him of all the positive things that were waiting to be experienced and enjoyed. This doesn't mean that he took no notice of the negative things around him. He noticed them, certainly, but he focused his time and attention only on the positive.

What an awesome responsibility the spies had, making their report to Moses. How they handled it would affect the next stage in Israelite history. What they said and how they said it would either stimulate or suffocate the faith and zeal of the entire nation. A positive report would spur them on to great things in God. Fear and negativism would act only as a damper.

At first, the spies were very positive: 'Yes, it *is* a land flowing with milk and honey. Everything God has said is true! Everything he promised is there for the taking. But…!' They then went on to explain about the giants who would stand in their way when they set out to conquer Canaan.

Notice there were no lies in what they reported. Everything they said was fact. There *were* great walled cities and there *were* giants. However, the majority of those spies allowed their fear to make them exaggerate the facts: 'The land we explored devours those living in it. All the people we saw there are of a great size' (Numbers 13:32).

In reality, the giants occupied only a small area in the south of the country. It was true that their presence would make Canaan's conquest more difficult, but not impossible. In fact, once the other inhabitants of Canaan had learned that the Israelites could destroy the giants, they would probably fall over themselves to surrender out of sheer terror! Sadly, the majority of spies focused on the only negative factor, and allowed this to drag themselves and the rest of the nation down into despair and unbelief: 'And they said to each other, "We should choose a leader and go back to Egypt" ' (Numbers 14:4).

Not Caleb, however! His positive attitude helped him to see beyond the problem to the potential. He knew that the benefits of going ahead in God and winning would eventually outweigh the difficulties and danger. He could probably already picture it in his mind. So rather than ignore or deny the problem, he simply looked beyond it with eyes of faith. 'Never mind the giants! Have you seen the size of the grapes?' In other words, 'Don't get hung up on the problem. Concentrate on the potential instead!' Having judged the situation positively in the light of God's promises, his attitude was, 'Let's do this in him. We are well able. Let's go for it now in God!' That's how confident his vision of the future was.

I don't know about you, but that's the kind of person I want to be. Potential-centred instead of problem-centred. I don't want to be bowed down any longer by the negatives in a situation. I want instead to be blessed by the abundance and beauty of the positives, which are there too, if I would only look for them. Like Caleb, I want to focus on the great potential that there is for me in God. I am tired of the rut, aren't you? Tired of the same old routine, the same old thoughts which flood into my head every time something unexpected or unpleasant happens, when I automatically fear the worst. Worse still are those dreaded 'What ifs' which haven't even happened yet, except in my imagination.

Have you ever wondered why Caleb's reaction was so different from that of the other spies? In a nutshell, God's promise made the difference, and the fact that Caleb wholeheartedly believed it. He was absolutely convinced that if God had said something, it was as good as done, whatever the problem, whatever the obstacles and the Lord God had very definitely given his word that Canaan would one day become their own possession (Exodus 3:8,17). The other spies had allowed their fear to crush their faith in that promise, but it is faith in God's unfailing promises which should always overcome the fear in us.

The Lord rewarded Caleb's faith. He is promised that he and his family will take ownership of every piece of ground over which he had walked as a spy in the hill country of Canaan. This was a tremendous promise, which Caleb undoubtedly believed. Have you noticed the setback, however? The promises were not to be fulfilled immediately. Caleb had to spend the next forty years wandering around the wilderness, surrounded by all those who had rebelled against God (Numbers 14:26–28).

I wonder what might have gone through his mind at that time? I wonder how he felt about having to wait until the last Israelite out of hundreds of thousands in his generation had died before he could receive his reward from God? Through no fault of his own, Caleb had

to stifle his zeal for another four decades, which is almost as long as I've been breathing. Had it been me, I think I would have been a little bit frustrated and annoyed about this. I would certainly be voicing rather loudly how unfair it all was! Not Caleb, however. Over the next forty years, he shows himself to be a man of patient faith.

I believe that many times during his years of wandering in that dry, dusty, monotonous wilderness, Caleb's thoughts were focused on the beautiful mountains of Canaan, where they had picked the huge cluster of grapes (Numbers 13:23). The fruit had long since gone, but the memory of it and the delicious taste were still firmly fixed in his mind. How often did he picture himself back there, enjoying the beauty and richness? How many nights did he lie awake in his tent, making his plans in God, thinking what he was going to do when he took possession of all that had been promised? For forty years, he dreamed his dream in God.

As Moses' successor, Joshua finally led the Israelites over the Jordan into the promised land. Battles were fought and enemies driven out, and they were established in God's sight as a nation. Sections of land were then allocated to the various families according to the traditional practice of drawing lots. No one was permitted to state their own preference. Instead, they accepted what was given them as the Lord's choice for them. Caleb and his family, however, had no need to participate. They knew already where God had chosen for them to settle. In absolute confidence and faith, Caleb, now eighty-five years old, steps forward to ask his friend Joshua to fulfil the divine promise made to him nearly half a century before (Joshua 14:6–15).

> Then Joshua blessed Caleb son of Jephunneh and gave
> him Hebron as his inheritance. So Hebron has belonged
> to Caleb son of Jephunneh the Kenizzite ever since,
> because he followed the Lord, the God of Israel, whole-
> heartedly.
>
> *(Joshua 14:13,14)*

As that battered, old taxi struggled to carry us high into the mountains of Africa, I realised that had Caleb not kept his eyes raised above ground level on that first journey into Canaan, he would have had nothing worthwhile to dream about over the years. By the end of my trip, and on every visit to Tanzania since, I have made myself look up and around me instead of constantly scanning the road, with the result that I too am like a child in a toy shop – absolutely delighted by what I see. What's a bit of goats' mess when the sunsets and scenery are so beautiful? By fixing my eyes on Jesus Christ, I find that I am less bogged down by all the negatives around me. I can now enjoy the many, many positives which come through knowing him. In fact, this year I have seen a childhood dream of my own come true in God. What is it? You have it in your hands now!

So go on. Don't be afraid. Dream your dreams in God. They can come true at just the right time. Honestly!

Focus

Thank the Lord for the dreams he has already fulfilled in your life thus far.

Now set before him those that have not yet come true. Ask yourself honestly if they have been birthed in you by the Holy Spirit or if they are simply a product of your own human desires. Commit each dream which is sincerely of God into his keeping, trusting him to make it come true at exactly the right time in him. Ask for the Holy Spirit's help to give you patient faith as you wait.

Feed

Joseph, second youngest son of Jacob, is his father's favourite. Life as he knows it is about to change for him.

Read Genesis chapters 37 and 39.

- What were the 'giants' in Joseph's life which stood in the way of him receiving the fulfilment of his dream?

Now read Genesis 41 and 42.

- How does Joseph's dream finally come true?
- What are the 'giants' that stand in the way of your own dream coming true?
- Do you believe that God can help you overcome them?

14

GOD'S ROAD MAP

Being footloose and fancy-free (my brother-in-law's description of my blessed state of singleness, to which he then adds, 'Jammy beggar!') allows me both the time and the freedom to spend most of my summer holidays from school on a cheap but cheerful campsite somewhere on the Continent (and very pleasant it is, too). I have to say, though, that it isn't all holiday. I do spend time studying, researching and writing, of course. At least, that's my excuse. Exactly where I end up, however, depends on the direction in which the Holy Spirit tells us to point the car when we get off the ferry in France.

Two years ago, we visited Portugal and Northern Spain – a round trip of almost 3,000 miles. We travelled by car, which was quite a challenge especially in the mountain regions. I should say, really, that we took Jenny's car. My own, known affectionately as 'RB' (short for 'Rust Bucket') struggles up the hill to the nearby town of Heanor most weeks, so what it would be like in the mist-covered mountains of Spain makes me panic just thinking about it! Even in Jenny's car, which is a 'baby' in comparison, there were some days when we found ourselves taking a deep breath and praying that the Lord would send a few broad-shouldered angels to give us a bit of a push. We made it, however, and it was well worth the effort. The scenery was wonderful, and so were those three other delightful 'S' words – sun, sea and sand!

You can imagine that travelling so far, Jenny and I had to spend many hours crammed together in the front of the car, the back being absolutely jammed full of camping equipment and luggage. As a firm believer in being comfortable while under canvas, I pack everything but the kitchen sink. (If I knew how to dismantle that, it would probably come along as well!) Praise God that he has blessed us with such a good friendship, because on these long trips it is often put to the test!

The majority of the time, Jenny drives and I sit alongside as navigator, road map poised, ready to tell her where to go – politely, of course! What undoubtedly happens, however, is that at some point on our travels, I find myself having to announce that I think we are lost and, being Christians, full of patience and love, the conversation which then takes place between us usually sounds like this:

Navigator:	Eh, Jenny…
Driver:	Yes, m'duck?
Navigator:	I'm afraid I have some bad news for you.
Driver:	What's that, sunshine?
Navigator:	I'm sorry, but we seem to be lost. I can't seem to find where we are on the map.
Driver:	Lost, m'duck? No! You could never manage to get us lost. You're much too clever for that! I'm sure you know exactly where we are. You're just kidding! 'S that right?
Navigator:	Sorry, sunbeam. I'm not kidding. I'm afraid we really are lost. I haven't seen any road signs for ages now. Oh dear, I hope I haven't caused you any problems! I'd understand if you were cross with me.
Driver:	Now, how could I be cross with a good friend like you? Just take another look at the map and I'm sure you'll sort it all out very soon.

OK, OK, so the conversation isn't usually as calm and polite! Perhaps a more honest account would sound something like this:

Driver:	Lost? Lost? What do you mean we're lost? Haven't you been looking at the map?
Navigator:	Of course, I've been looking at it! All morning to be exact! And all you've done is drive! If you'd just slow down long enough for me to read some of the road signs, I'd get on a whole lot better!
Driver:	Oh, so it's my fault, is it? That's just typical. You get us lost and all of a sudden it's the driver's fault! And, pray tell me, exactly

	when was the last time you knew where we were?
Navigator:	About two miles back – right about the time you drove straight through that 'Stop' sign.
Driver:	'Stop' sign? What 'Stop' sign? I didn't see any 'Stop' sign!
Navigator:	Exactly. It's a wonder we weren't both killed!
Driver:	Look, I can't do everything at once. I can't possibly be expected to drive *and* watch for road signs at the same time. I just didn't see it, OK?
Navigator:	Huh! A blind man could have seen it!
Driver:	Or one with eyes in the back of his head, perhaps? Is that what you think I have? Eyes in the back of my head? If I had eyes in the back of my head, I wouldn't need you to navigate!
Navigator:	Well, if that's how you feel, do it yourself next time!

That's usually how it ends up when we get lost, isn't it? We panic and become annoyed because we don't like to feel that we have somehow lost control. And have you noticed that it is always someone else's fault, never our own?

Losing our way abroad has become a habit with Jenny and I, even though we are well practised in the art of driving on the Continent. (In fact, have I mentioned that any major European city in which we haven't been lost just isn't worth visiting?) There may be many genuine reasons why this happens. Sometimes we fail to hear the navigator's instructions until it is too late, or sometimes we decide that we know better than the road map and we devise our own route instead.

Over the years, I have come to realise just how important road maps have become in our society. We wouldn't be able to travel the world without them. They are vital in my life, especially during our annual camping expeditions, when hardly a day goes by without us having to consult them. It is the same on that greater journey in which each of us is involved at present – our journey through life. From the day we are conceived, through birth and on until we take our place in eternity, we are travelling on a spiritual journey. And God has a plan (a road map, if you like) for each of us as we travel through life.

'For I know the plans I have for you,' declares the Lord,
'plans to prosper you and not to harm you, plans to give
you hope and a future.'

(Jeremiah 29:11)

In his plan, God has expressed everything that he would like to happen
to us on our journey through life. There is a different plan for each of
us – his plan for your life is not the same as his plan for mine or anyone else's. We were created as individuals and that is how the Lord
treats us.

I will instruct you and teach you in the way you should go;
I will counsel you and watch over you.

(Psalm 32:8)

The Holy Spirit is the navigator on our journey through life. As we
keep looking to him and listening to his directions, he will consult
each individual 'map' and tell us the best way to go. As we set aside
time to talk and to listen to him, he will reveal the next little section
in his plan. The more time we spend with him, the more familiar his
voice becomes and the more obvious his directions.

The watchman opens the gate for him [the shepherd],
and the sheep listen to his voice. He calls his own sheep
by name and leads them out. When he has brought out
all his own, he goes on ahead of them, and his sheep follow him because they know his voice.

(John 10:3–4)

O people of Zion … you will weep no more. How gracious
he will be when you cry for help! As soon as he hears, he
will answer you … Whether you turn to the right or to
the left, your ears will hear a voice behind you, saying,
'This is the way; walk in it.'

(Isaiah 30:19,21)

Jesus himself declares:

'I am the way and the truth and the life. No-one comes to
the Father except through me.'

(John 14:6)

So we are guided on our journey through life by faith and trust in

Jesus. In his life, death and resurrection, he offers the only signpost to point us back to our Creator. Fixing our eyes on him and following where the Holy Spirit leads will take us to our final destination – eternity with God.

Have you ever wondered why the Lord never shows us his whole plan at one time? Why does he give us a few directions only each day, so that the plan is revealed gradually, piece by piece? The answer is very simple. He reveals his plan in small sections because our human minds could not cope with any more than that. When we are in the front seat of a car, navigating, how do we have the map? Completely unfolded and stretched out before us? I don't think so! The driver would struggle to manoeuvre the gears or to see properly out of the windscreen. When we cannot manage with the whole map unravelled at the one time, what do we tend to do? We fold it, don't we, into a size that is easier to cope with. When it becomes a more manageable size, all we can see is where we are now, where we have just come from and only a little of where we are headed towards – and that is enough for now. Then, as we go, we unfold another piece, and another piece, and so on. Better still, we buy a map book which is already divided, page by page, into manageable sections.

Believe it or not, this is exactly what the Lord does with us. He knows that our finite minds can cope with only a little at a time, so that is all he reveals day by day. What we must never forget, however, is that although we can't see the whole plan – the whole road ahead of us – the Lord can. He has the whole map for each of our lives already stretched out in front of him, and he is ready always to consult it and give us directions.

This reminds me of a very common scene often depicted in many of the old black-and-white World War II films that feature an RAF Operations room. Laid out on a table in the centre of the room is a map of Europe showing the positions of RAF planes already in action. As each position alters, the Operations team marks each change on the map so that those giving the orders know exactly what is happening at each stage of their strategy. In the same way, the Holy Spirit has stretched out in front of him the whole 'map' and strategy information for each of our lives.

So, during the times when you are not sure of what is happening and where you are going to end up, don't panic. The Lord knows exactly what is going on and he is totally in control. Keep listening. Keep looking for the signs. Keep following his directions in faith and in trust, and you will achieve and enjoy all God has planned for you in his wisdom and in love.

Focus

David's words in Psalm 32:9 paint a picture of a horse and a mule which have to be guided by means of a bit and bridle. Imagine a mule having to be dragged, pushed or prodded before it will move.

Ask the Holy Spirit to remind you of times in the past when you have been as 'stubborn as a mule' in response to God's commands. How did the Father deal with you then? Did he use a 'big stick' to prod you onwards? What are his perfect means of motivation – fear or love?

Feed

Read Matthew 6:24–34.

These words of Jesus form part of his sermon on the mount.

- In your own words, write down what Jesus is saying here. Draw out his specific promises to his followers. Speaking aloud, claim each one as your own.
- Notice that the promise given in verse 33 carries with it a condition. What is this?
- Read verse 34 again in the light of these words of Corrie Ten Boom:*

  Worry does not empty tomorrow of its sorrow, it empties today of its strength.

Note

*   From *Clippings from my Notebook*

15

WHERE TO NOW, LORD?

Picture the scene. One small hatchback car packed to the gunnels with everything needed for a comfortable camping holiday abroad (except for the kitchen sink, of course!). Hundreds of impatient Spaniards all trying to drive home in rush-hour traffic. Two very hot and hassled British tourists trying frantically to find the road south out of the Spanish city of Seville. Jenny, the Welsh one sitting behind the steering wheel, keeps glancing sideways at her navigator, hoping desperately to hear that wonderfully liberating phrase, 'That away!', accompanied by an equally wonderful pointing finger raised to show the road out of this waking nightmare. All around is raging the cacophony of blaring car horns and irate, gesticulating Spanish drivers. Jeanette, the Scottish one, is perched like a pregnant parrot on the absolute edge of her seat, head pushed precariously out through the open window, scrutinising each passing signpost as if her life depended on it, searching for directions to Spain's seemingly most elusive destination, Malaga. There are signs showing the way to each of the many museums and art galleries. There is even a signpost pointing the way north to Spain's illustrious capital, Madrid, thousands of kilometres away. But a sign directing weary travellers south to sunny Malaga? No way, José! Or, as they say in my part of the world, 'In your dreams, pal!'

Round and round we drove, becoming more and more despondent. Ironically, we knew that the rest of our journey south was fairly straightforward. The road map revealed clear information about the type of terrain that awaited us, the number of kilometres still to be covered, and so on. The problem, however, was how to get off this urban roundabout. Should we take the first available escape route out of Seville, relieving the hassle of irate drivers but risking heading in the opposite direction to where we wanted to go? Or should we wait for the crucial road sign, which we obviously kept missing, to suddenly come out of hiding?

We prayed silently, asking the Lord, who knew exactly where we were and exactly where we needed to be, to direct us out and onward. Ten minutes later, stuck in yet another tailback of traffic, I just 'happened' to glance over to where a gang of workmen were digging up a long section of tarmac, ready to lay some kind of piping. I can remember thinking to myself, 'I could murder an ice cream!', when I saw it – the words 'MALAGA N334', followed by a large black arrow indicating the first turn-off to the left. Relieved, we obeyed its instructions and before long we were on the open road again, with everything calm and peaceful.

Why had such a crucial road sign evaded us for so long? You won't believe it, but this so-called crucial 'signpost' was no more than a scribble of untidy letters painted on the back of an old dustbin lid which was then tied with string to one end of a splintered broom handle. The other end was rammed unceremoniously into an upturned milk crate! The 'official' sign was lying on top of a pile of rubble waiting to be re-erected by the workmen once their excavations were over. We weren't impressed, I can tell you!

Remembering the frustration involved in some of my travels abroad makes me reflect on my journey through life. Does the same stress and confusion meet me when I am seeking guidance from God? When the Holy Spirit consults God's 'road map' for my life and then tells me the best way to go, are his directions always clear and obvious, leaving no room for error? Looking back, I would have to confess that during the most significant changes in my life, the Lord's instructions and the 'signposts' he places along the way, have been clear. Admittedly, these have been times when I have genuinely been seeking God's will for my future.

In 2 Samuel 5:17–25, we are told that the mighty Philistine army, David's fiercest enemies, were determined to attack and destroy him. So far his forces had managed to elude them, but David knew that this could not go on for ever. So he asks the Lord two very specific questions, (1) 'Shall I go and attack the Philistines? and (2) 'Will you hand them over to me?' In response, he receives two equally specific replies: (1) 'Go!' and (2) 'for I will surely hand [them] over to you' (v19). And that is exactly what happened! David followed the Lord's instructions and won a tremendous military victory as a result.

The Lord often gives us 'signposts' to help us navigate our way through life. In my own experience, there are many examples. Towards the end of 1980, my course at the local teacher training college was nearing an end and I was due to graduate the following summer. At the time, these words from Isaiah seemed especially significant:

'See, the former things have taken place,
  and new things I declare;
before they spring into being
  I announce them to you.'

(Isaiah 42:9)

Then, without any prompting on my part, other Christians, whom I trust in the Lord, began sharing with me how they believed that I should be seeking God about going to Bible college – yet another sign-post pointing the way ahead. My response? 'No way! I'm just finishing three years of hard study at the TTC. No way am I going back to study books so quickly! I'm going to settle down, get a position in teaching, make some money and live a little!' That was *my* plan; the Lord, how-ever, had other ideas.

Then, along with over one hundred fellow graduates, I discovered that there were no teaching jobs available in our region at that time, because of severe cuts in educational funding. Again, I went to the Lord, asking him to reveal the next part of his road map for my life. Again, Christian friends reassured me that they felt God would open the way for me to go to Bible college. So I continued to pray and began to find out what the various theological colleges had to offer.

To cut a long story short (OK, who said 'Hallelujah!'?), because I had already been accepted by Child Evangelism Fellowship to train at the Leadership Institute in Switzerland for three months, I was limit-ed in the choice of colleges I could attend – most of the courses would have already started before I returned to Britain. In fact, only two with later starting dates remained – the Baptist Training Institute in Glasgow and Moorlands Bible College way down in the south of England. If I tell you that at the time I was living in Scotland, not many miles from Edinburgh, and only a short train journey from Glasgow, what would have been your natural choice of college? Having learned from past experience, however, that God does not necessarily go for the obvious course of action, I prayed for clear guidance: (1) 'Am I to go to Bible college this year, Lord?' and (2) 'If so, which one?'

The Lord answered very quickly through that particular day's read-ing in the notes I was using at the time:

Now an angel of the Lord said to Philip, 'Go south...'

(Acts 8:26)

Now this instruction was, of course, directed specifically to Philip, and I would not usually read something like this and assume that it meant *I* should go south. But because I'd been praying so specifically, 'North or South, Lord?', this verse leaped off the page at me in a remarkable way, and I knew the Lord had spoken.

I hope I have demonstrated by this example the many ways in which the Lord can give us his 'signposts' to guide us: through the Bible, through the words and prayers of other Christians, through the way circumstances work out as doors open or close for us. We should constantly be on the look out, expecting God's guidance in every aspect of our lives, whether it be where we are to go next in our jobs or careers, down to the most personal concern, however great or small. The Lord is a wonderful navigator, always ready to direct when we are sincerely ready to listen and obey. He will always have our best interests at heart. (Had I not gone to Moorlands, I would never have met my friend and co-worker, Jenny, and the next part in the divine plan for my own life and Jenny's would have been seriously delayed.)

So the Holy Spirit navigator certainly knows what he is doing. Trust him. Listen to him. Obey his commands. You will be amazed at where, why and how he leads you!

Focus

> When a man's ways are pleasing to the Lord,
> he makes even his enemies live at peace with him.
>
> *(Proverbs 16:7)*

Prayerfully, consider the ways you now find yourself walking along at present. Are they pleasing to the Lord? Ask for the Holy Spirit's help to reveal anything which displeases him, and confess these.

Now ask for the Lord's supernatural help in recognising his 'signposts' as soon as they appear in your life, eg unexpected changes in circumstances, words of scripture, the confirmation of at least two or three other Christians, and so on.

Feed

Under Joshua's leadership, the Israelites continue their journey through the wilderness towards the promised land of Canaan. Just outside the great walled city of Jericho, the next part of God's plan for them is revealed. It is vital that they conquer this mighty stronghold if they are to continue. But how are they to achieve this?

Read Joshua 6:1–21.
- What were the people instructed to do on the following days?

Day 1)	Did they obey?
Day 2)	Did they obey?
Day 3)	Did they obey?
Day 4)	Did they obey?
Day 5)	Did they obey?
Day 6)	Did they obey?
Day 7)	Did they obey?

- Had they done exactly the same on Day 7 as they had done on Day 6, what do you think would have happened? Why?

- What was the result of their willing obedience?

16

SPIRITUAL EARPLUGS?

I was very impressed recently while watching one of the regular holiday programmes on television. It featured some well-known celebrities sharing what they consider to be the five most essential items required when travelling abroad. Most of them mentioned the obvious – electric travel plug, travel iron, travel kettle, hair-dryer, lap-top, electronic notebook, mobile phone, etc, etc. All very predictable and boring. One journalist, however, revealed that he never travels overseas without taking a spare sink-and-bath plug with him (I'm serious!), and he promptly opened up his shaving case and produced them. Seemingly, he finds these missing in the majority of foreign hotel rooms he stays in. (The things some people will pinch!)

Top of my own list of 'Basic Travel Essentials' will probably surprise you. When I'm getting ready to travel abroad (especially to Africa), one of the first things I pack is – wait for it – a pair of earplugs! And the second most vital item to be included in my luggage? A spare pair of earplugs! Why? Whenever we visit Dar-es-Salaam, the local Christians, our hosts, usually organise for us to stay in a hotel run by the nearby parish church, which always seems to have something to celebrate, praise God! Wedding receptions, confirmation parties, anniversary gatherings are all held outside in the hotel courtyard, which all the guest bedrooms both overlook and overhear. And, boy, do those Africans know how to celebrate – usually very loudly until three or four o'clock in the morning!

Because we have to follow a very hectic schedule when we are there – teaching in the churches, visiting people's homes to share the gospel, praying for the sick, counselling those who need advice and encouragement and so on (all of which we count as a privilege from God) – we find that in order to be energetically efficient (and enthusiastic) in the African heat, we need to have a long and restful sleep every night. And how do we guarantee that? We each wear a pair of earplugs! Small and seemingly insignificant they may appear, but they are a must if I'm to snore the whole night through (which, incidentally, is another reason for Jenny having to wear them). I should say also that it isn't just the city which is noisy at night. High in the mountains, where there is no electricity never mind noisy parties, what would keep me awake if I didn't wear earplugs would be the din of the crickets and the sound of the bats crashing through the trees outside. So earplugs are vitally essential on my travels, because they dull annoying and unwanted noise, whatever that may be.

Now, believe it or not, there is a very relevant link between earplugs, God's road map and our spiritual journey through life. Puzzled? Then let me explain. When the Holy Spirit consults the divine 'route map' for our lives and tells us the best way to go, there are times, if we are honest, when we fail to obey. Either we don't hear the Lord's directions clearly enough or we wilfully choose to ignore them and go our own way instead. Whatever the reason, the outcome is always the same: we end up on the wrong road, well and truly *lost*, missing out on all the good things God had planned for us. Why does this happen? The simplest explanation is that we have 'stopped up' the 'ears of our spirit' with spiritual 'earplugs'. We have deliberately dulled the sound of the Holy Spirit's voice asking us to follow him.

'Me? Wear earplugs? Rubbish!' you may say – but let me now refer to these spiritual ear-stoppers by their more familiar names: *busyness*, when the noise of the world and all its demands shuts out the voice of the Holy Spirit ; *procrastination*, the so-called 'thief of time' which cries, 'Don't worry – tomorrow will do'; *unconfessed sin*, which eventually desensitises the heart; *half-heartedness in seeking God's will*, when we fail to follow fully because we are only half listening to his instructions; *creative excuse-making*, when anything of our own invention seems preferable to the particularly difficult 'stretch of road' which the divine road map may be indicating. How many of us can deny the presence of some of these in our lives? How often have they caused a delay or unnecessary diversion on our spiritual journey? Embarrassingly, I have to admit that over the years, procrastination has been the means by which I have most often dulled the Spirit's voice in my life. I have succumbed to this so often that a friend has announced that my epitaph will read: 'This is one thing she couldn't put off until tomorrow'!

Recently, I was challenged by some verses in the book of Numbers:

When Moses sent them to explore Canaan, he said, 'Go up
through the Negev and on into the hill country. See what
the land is like and whether the people who live there are
strong or weak, few or many. What kind of land do they
live in? Is it good or bad? What kind of towns do they live
in? Are they unwalled or fortified? How is the soil? Is it
fertile or poor? Are there trees on it or not? Do your best
to bring back some of the fruit of the land.' (It was the
season for the first ripe grapes.)

(Numbers 13:17–20)

Here we see just how important timing is in any plan which God draws
up. The twelve spies are sent out (v 20) in the 'season of the first grapes'
(the end of July) when the very best fruit was in evidence. They are told
to bring back samples of the local produce. If they had waited too long
before setting out, the fruit would have been past its best and they
would not have had a true indication of how fertile the land really was.

There is a time for everything,
　　and a season for every activity under heaven:
a time to be born and a time to die,
　　a time to plant and a time to uproot,
　　a time to kill and a time to heal,
　　a time to tear down and a time to build,
　　a time to weep and a time to laugh,
　　a time to mourn and a time to dance,
　　a time to scatter stones and a time to gather them,
　　a time to embrace and a time to refrain,
　　a time to search and a time to give up,
　　a time to keep and a time to throw away,
　　a time to tear and a time to mend,
　　a time to be silent and a time to speak,
　　a time to love and a time to hate,
　　a time for war and a time for peace.

(Ecclesiastes 3:1–8)

There is a specific time for everything in life. In God's plan for each of
us, his timing is perfect and we do well to adhere to it. To hesitate in following his guidance can mean that we hinder the efficiency of his plan
and ruin our true potential in Christ. In the end, it was disobedience
rather than procrastination which caused the Israelites to end up on the
wrong road, and they spent the next four decades wandering through
the wilderness instead of enjoying the benefits and blessings of Canaan.

Now I can't leave things there without asking what happens when we do find ourselves getting lost on our spiritual journey: perhaps because we have become distracted by other things and have failed to hear the Holy Spirit's directions; perhaps because we haven't dealt with sin and it has become a barrier standing in the way of our going on with God; perhaps because we have stubbornly decided that we know better than anyone and we have gone our own way instead, ending up in the wrong place at the wrong time, missing out on blessing because we are not in the right place to receive it.

On holiday, when Jenny and I found ourselves heading in the wrong direction, we used to react wrongly. We used to keep on driving round and round in circles, hoping to catch sight of something, a sign or road marking, to help us find our way again. (I think we secretly hoped that a direction sign would suddenly leap out in front of us and yell, 'Oi! You two! This way!' But it never did.) All that happened was that we ended up driving around endlessly in vain, getting more and more frustrated and angry. Now, however, it's very different. As soon as we realise that we are lost, we pull in at the side of the road and take a closer look at the map to try and work out where we went wrong in the first place, because when we know that, we can then work out how to get back on to the right road again.

When we find ourselves 'lost' on our spiritual journey through life and are missing out on God's potential and blessings, let's not make the mistake of going round and round in spiritual 'circles', hoping that everything will somehow sort itself out. Let's stop and, in humility, go back to the Lord, confessing our sin, our procrastination, our over-busyness, and asking him to show us where he now wants us to be. You won't be alone in this. Some of the mightiest men in scripture have had to do just that before the Lord could lead them back on to the road that would bring him greatest glory.

Is this how you find yourself these days – lost spiritually and struggling on your journey through life? What is the cause? Stubbornness? Fear? Half-heartedness? Unconfessed sin? Whatever the reason, don't be thinking, 'That's it! I've blown it now! Might as well resign myself to missing out on all the good things of God. It's what I deserve.' I'm very pleased to be able to say that this is not what the Lord is thinking.

> 'For I know the plans I have for you,' declares the Lord,
> 'plans to prosper you and not to harm you, plans to give
> you hope and a future. Then you will call upon me and
> come and pray to me, and I will listen to you. You will
> seek me and find me when you seek me with all your

heart. I will be found by you,' declares the Lord, 'and will bring you back from captivity.'

(Jeremiah 29:11–14)

So don't give up. Instead, *stop*! Go back and ask the Lord to show you where you went wrong in the first place. How did you end up on the wrong road? Tell him how sorry you are that you are not where you should be in Christ. Ask for the Holy Spirit's help to find the right road again. Then wait, listen, follow his directions, and may you soon be achieving and enjoying once again all that the Lord wants to pour so richly into your life each day!

Focus

Consider your life at present. Are you wearing spiritual 'earplugs'? If so, identify their more familiar name.

How have they diverted or hindered you on your spiritual journey thus far? Confess them. Receive the Lord's forgiveness and cleansing. Ask the Holy Spirit to direct you on the right road again.

Feed

Jesus and his disciples are on their way from the upper room to the Mount of Olives where he is about to be betrayed by Judas' kiss.

- Read Mark 14:27–30. Which emotions do you think prompted Peter's hasty declaration?

Jesus has been arrested and taken to the high priest's home. Peter waits covertly in the courtyard.

- Read Luke 22:54–62. Which emotions now prompted Peter's denial? How do you think he would feel afterwards?

It is now after the resurrection. Jesus has been waiting for the disciples on the seashore. He shares a meal with them and then has a discussion with Peter.

- Read John 21:15–19. What does Jesus express to Peter here?

Jesus has ascended into heaven. Peter and John have just healed a man who had been crippled from birth. They are arrested and brought before the council of Israel's highest court of law.

- Read Acts 4:1–23. How does God allow Peter to make amends for his earlier denial?
- Do you so graciously allow those who have failed or hurt you to make amends?

17

SUCH STYLE!

Picture the scene. Six a.m. on an already sweltering morning on board an African ferry on Lake Tanganyika... I stood on deck with Pastor Meshak, our host, surveying the beautiful landscape and enjoying the antics of some nearby fishermen.

'Tell me,' said Meshak, 'have you ever sailed by ferryboat before?'

'Oh yes, many times,' I replied, remembering past camping holidays abroad. 'We travel often by ferry.'

'A ferryboat like this?' he asked proudly.

'No, much bigger!' I said, espying the handful of cabins and deck space for only one car.

'How much bigger?' he persisted.

'Oh, about ten times bigger, I suppose. They're so big that they have restaurants, shops, bars, and in some cases even cinemas on board!'

'No!' he cried with disbelief. 'This I cannot imagine! You are teasing me. Yes?'

'I'm not!' I replied, a little peeved.

'Then it is a miracle,' he declared, 'that something so big can stay on top of the water.'

'Huh! That's nothing,' I continued. 'Nowadays we don't need the top of the water at all. We can now travel beneath it!'

'Beneath it?!' His eyes were almost out of their sockets. 'You mean that you can walk beneath the sea?'

'Well, drive actually – or at least the train does. We just sit in our cars.'

'Trains? Cars? At the bottom of the sea? Now I know you are teasing! I think you see these things only with your imagination.'

'I've done more than that Meshak,' I retorted. 'I've actually seen them with my own eyes.'

I then explained about the Channel Tunnel and how it works. In the end I managed to convince Meshak that man is now able to do more than he can imagine. The conversation then turned to what the apostle Paul writes in his letter to the Ephesians:

> Now to him who is able to do immeasurably more than all we ask or imagine, according to his power that is at work within us, to him be glory in the church and in Christ Jesus throughout all generations, for ever and ever! Amen.
>
> *(Ephesians 3:20,21)*

Meshak admitted that he really was unsure what these words meant in relation to our lives as Christians. Within one month, however, the Holy Spirit showed him in practical ways exactly how this applies to daily living. I'll share one example with you.

Our visit to Africa was nearing its end. It was time to return to Burundi on the first stage of our journey home. Just before we sailed, we had news from Bujumbura, the capital. Fifteen more people had been killed by Tutsi rebels. Foreign missionaries were now planning to leave the city. However, we were assured by a Swedish missionary there that he would meet us at the port and take us to his guarded compound, where we would be safe until it was time to fly out. We arrived, however, to find that he had been delayed and there was no one to escort us safely through the town. For security reasons, we were advised not to trust the local taxi drivers.

So there we sat on the quayside, looking very conspicuous, everyone noticing we were there. I felt like an elephant at a dog show! As we waited, we talked to the Lord, our Protector, inviting him to step in and take control of the problem. We were amazed at how he chose to do this.

Also on the quayside were two African bodyguards. They had been sent by the Zairean Embassy to meet an important diplomat, but there was no sign of him – which in it itself was a little worrying! Rather than return empty-handed, they agreed to escort us instead, and let me tell you, they had come in a beautiful, white luxury limousine with a little Zairean flag on the front. So there we were, completely safe and comfortable, riding around like the Queen!

The Lord declares through his prophet Isaiah:

> 'So do not fear, for I am with you;
>   do not be dismayed, for I am your God.

Such style!

I will strengthen you and help you;
    I will uphold you with my righteous right hand.'

                                                       (Isaiah 41:10)

God, our Helper, had done us proud. He had solved the problem for us with such style! All we had asked for was safe transport to the other side of town. Anything would have done, even a rickety old bus, of which there are thousands in Africa. The Lord had indeed accomplished 'immeasurably more than all we had asked or imagined'. What a glorious, gracious and generous God he is!

Now to him who is able ... be glory in the church and in
Christ Jesus throughout all generations, for ever and
ever! Amen.

                                           (Ephesians 3:20,21)

Focus

Think back to the times in your life when God, in answering your prayers, has done far more than you ever asked for. Thank him for these and bear them in mind as you make your requests to him today.

Feed

Read John 6:1–14.

This is an eye-witness account of one of the 'signs' recorded in John's Gospel, 'that you may believe that Jesus is the Christ, the Son of God, and that by believing you may have life in his name' (John 20:31).

- Why were the crowds drawn to Jesus (6:1–4)? What drew you to him?
- How did Jesus test his disciples (6:5–10)?
- What evidence was there to show that Jesus had done far more than anyone could have imagined?

And my God will meet all your needs according to his
glorious riches in Christ Jesus.

                                           (Philippians 4:19)

Note that this verse does not say that God will meet your needs '*out of* his glorious riches' but '*according to* his glorious riches *in Christ Jesus*'. What difference should this statement make in your own life and expectations?

EPILOGUE

By now I hope that you are convinced that God is interested in every part of you, and wants to meet with you and teach you through the ordinary, everyday things around you. (It doesn't only happen to me!) Ironically, if I were asked to explain exactly how this works, I would have to confess that I'm not totally sure. I'm just glad that it does. All I can say is that some kind of special supernatural 'tuning process' takes place between our spirits and God's spirit, which he himself initiates at our request (he will never force this on us without our permission). Let me explain what I mean.

In Tanzania, because church meetings last so long, the children are allowed to play out of doors while their parents worship and listen to the word of God. One day, as I was teaching from the pulpit, a loud and tearful 'Mama!' was heard from somewhere outside. Now it could have been uttered by any one of a dozen children. But, amazingly, only one lady – the distressed child's mother – responded and went out to comfort him. No other mother (and there were many in church that day) moved. How did they know so quickly that it was not their own child crying? To me, most distressed children sound the same – and I'm a dinner lady often dealing with several in a day!

Later, when I asked the mother how she had known it was her child who had cried, she replied, 'I cannot explain it. I just knew deep inside that my son needed me, so I went to him. The bond I have with him is so strong, my heart is always aware of him even when my mind is busy with other things.' In a nutshell, what she was saying is that, as his parent, something deep inside her is constantly tuned in to something deep inside her child, even when she was not actively thinking of him. It had taken a while, but during the years since his birth this innate sensitivity had increased the more time they had spent in each other's company.

I am convinced that this same sensitivity (ie spiritual tuning-in) exists in the special, supernatural bond between God the Father and his children. The greater our desire just to be with him, enjoying his company (bringing no prayer requests or hidden agendas), the easier it becomes to recognise what he is saying through the ordinary experiences of life. Very often we learn spiritually through the everyday without being consciously aware of it, and the link between real-life events and what we are reading daily in scripture becomes more easily apparent.

This tuning-in process doesn't develop overnight. The Lord often tests our desire to meet with him in this way, so keep persevering. Keep on looking for God in the everyday. Write your own 'chapters', linking what you discover in your regular Bible reading with what you find happening around you. Keep on practising the presence of Jesus in your life. Take time out to focus on him and to feed on his word. And why not share the insights he gives you with others to encourage them in their own Christian walk? After all, that's what it's all about, isn't it?